THE INTERPRETER'S HANDBOOK

RUSSELL K. GRATER AUTHOR

EARL JACKSON EDITOR

Southwest Parks and Monuments Association

Library of Congress Catalog Card Number: 76-14116

SBN Number: 0-911408-40-1

First Printing, 1976, 10,000

Technical Series No. 8

Southwest Parks and Monuments Association

Printed in the United States of America

INTRODUCTION

PREFACE

This book is dedicated to my wife who, through the years, has understood my weaknesses and encouraged what strengths I have,

and to

Dr. Harold C. Bryant who did so much to make possible my work as an interpreter in the National Parks, and who helped instill in me some of the qualities I believe an interpreter should have.

What is Interpretation?

A visitor walked up to the desk in the Visitor Center and said: "Some one said this is an interpretive center, and that I could get my questions answered here. I don't know what an interpretive center is, but I do need some information."

This visitor was not unusual. Many people do not know what is meant by interpretation, and many more do not know what an interpreter is. To some it is simply a fancy new word. However, slowly but surely, this work is becoming better known and appreciated by the public. For that reason, it is important that the person who selects the field of interpretation as a career should become as familiar as possible with the subject, and how it can be successfully accomplished.

The question is often asked: "What is the difference between interpretation and information? Don't they mean the same, with just different words being used?" Unfortunately, this conception is often accepted by the person meeting the public in our parks, before clubs and organizations, or in related situations. Many a guided tour is simply a vocal listing of facts and figures about what is being seen. There may be some minor interpretation accomplished, but it is lost in the maze of details. It is likely that you have gone on a tour through a dam, a power plant, a museum, an important building, or a park, and came away with your head so whirling with facts and figures that your mind could not begin to retain them, let alone understand what they really meant.

Interpretation differs from information in many basic respects. *"Interpretation,"* by contrast with information, conveys the meaning of something, through exposition or explanation. *"Information"* is the knowledge derived from study, experience, or instruction. It is information that is so often given to a visitor; it is interpretation that should have been accomplished. Good interpretation uses all sorts of information such as facts, figures, etc., but in a way that the listener can understand and appreciate.

If we put into simple words the end results we hope to accomplish through interpretation, they would be: Understand, stimulate and appreciate. Let us examine these words carefully to grasp the meaning of each. A person can be a good listener without understanding a thing. Without understanding, any explanation is sterile from the listener viewpoint.

With understanding may come a desire in the listener to learn more about what is being discussed. If you accomplish this, you have succeeded in another of your objectives, stimulating him to try on his own to enlarge his knowledge of the subject.

With understanding and desire to learn more comes a sense of appreciation of the subject, and what its worth really is. This doesn't mean appreciation cannot be had without understanding and stimulation; simply that it is greatly enhanced in combination with the other two factors. One can appreciate a view of the Grand Canyon and not understand or want to learn a thing about it. However, still greater appreciation is likely to accompany an understanding of how the great canyon came to be, with a desire to learn more of its story.

Anyone can be an interpreter if he is familiar with the story to be told, and with methods and techniques of interpretation that can make the story come alive and meaningful.

INTRODUCTION

For more than 33 years, I have been involved with the problems of interpretation, mostly in the National Parks and Monuments throughout the United States. Time spent in the field has only underscored the fact that it is a broad subject, and no one can expect to contact all of its many facets. Yet the years have definitely disclosed certain basic patterns that, if followed, insure a desired result. Interpretive methods, skills and techniques are constantly improving. New devices are being produced, so one cannot simply select one medium and say "this is the best." The media selected are only the best he knows about until better ones come along.

In this book I have recorded those things that have proved themselves through the years. I consider them basic to sound interpretation, and all can be built upon without question as to their worth. Because these methods, skills and techniques were, in large measure, developed in the many parks of our country—National, State and local—examples will mostly come from these sources.

This book, then, is primarily directed toward those persons who do interpretive work in the natural, historical, archeological and recreation parks, forests and museums of our country, although the methods and techniques described are equally effective in many activities and situations where interpretation is to be accomplished.

I am especially appreciative of the many ways in which interpreters in the National and State parks over the country have aided me through the years in my efforts to become an accomplished field naturalist and interpreter. It is not possible here to mention all of them, but the names of such pioneer interpreters as Edwin D. McKee, "Bert" Harwell, "Ed" Beatty, Natt Dodge, Doug Hubbard, Frank Brockman, George Ruhle, Ben Gale, Louis Schellbach, Howard Stagner, Carl Russell, Bill Carr, Earl Jackson and Paul Covell quickly come to mind. Others are presently making their own contributions to new ways of interpreting their areas. Many of their time-proven methods have been incorporated in this book.

Designing the Interpretive Program

CHAPTER 1
Qualities of a Good Interpreter

There is an old saying that "By their fruits you shall know them." Certainly this applies to an interpreter, as there are definite characteristics he should have to deal effectively with the public.

Friendliness is, without doubt, the key to all good interpretation. There is something very negative about walking up to a person, and being met with a frown or an emotionless face. Here again, there comes into play another old saying: "First impressions don't wait; they cannot be postponed." The way in which you greet the visitor; the way you act in taking over a group; the way you present a talk; everything you do, in fact, contributes toward creating an impression in the other person's mind. If these impressions are good, the chances are he will be eager to listen to you. If not, he will more than likely tend to draw back mentally, thus blocking out what you are trying to say. There is something appealing about a friendly greeting and smile which tends to break down any reserve the visitor may have, and get you started on the right foot. It is a tough job to get a good working relationship with a person (or group) once you have created a mental coolness in him. No matter how well you know the story you are telling, something vital has gone if he listens with reserved politeness. Of course, being friendly does not mean being effusive and a "glad-hander." This can also create the opposite impression from what is desired. Frequently a visitor is in your area for the first time, and not exactly certain what he wants to do or know. He may be somewhat reluctant to walk up to you and ask questions, even if you are obviously there for that purpose. This is especially true if you are in uniform, as a uniform sometimes has certain implications to the visitor. Thus, if he is met with a friendly manner, he is put at ease immediately, and likely will be receptive to what you have to tell him. The same is true with an audience. When you come out on stage, there is likely to be a feeling of formality in the air; a feeling it is essential to dispel. A smile can go a long way toward accomplishing this. Be friendly, whether you want to succeed as an interpreter, a salesman or a ditch digger! It pays off!

Another important characteristic of the good interpreter is an interest in the visitor or listener. A cool, impersonal approach likely will insure a similar attitude on the other person's part. In my experience almost everyone responds to an obvious interest in how he is enjoying his visit, where he comes from, and what he has been doing while in the area. Many visitors are eager to talk to someone, and all enjoy mention of their home town or state. The interpreter who knows something about the visitor's home region has little difficulty in developing rapport. Naturally, interest in the visitor does not mean being a "Paul Pry" into his affairs. Simply be a good listener as the visitor talks. It is a most valuable asset.

Earnestness and sincerity are vital. There are many ways of telling about something, and the way your presentation is received depends in large measure upon these qualities in you. If the listener feels that you are simply spouting routine, that you have said the same thing a thousand times to others, and are just doing a job, be assured your message will not be likely to receive the interest it should. People know when you are trying to make your message interesting to them.

Be helpful. The interpreter who goes a step beyond what the visitor expects is doing his job as it should be done. Sometimes helpfulness is not appreciated, or you think it isn't, but it can never hurt.

Be neat. This is especially important if you wear a uniform. People expect a uniform to appear well cared for and presentable at all times. A visitor may be hot, uncomfortable, dusty, wearing a dirty shirt or trousers that need pressing, but he expects you to be cool, relaxed and well groomed. A shirt with perspiration rings, a tie that should have been discarded some time ago, trousers that need cleaning—these can badly weaken anything you are trying to do for the visiting public. If you wear a uniform, wear it with pride!

There is a mistaken idea that a good interpreter must be a polished orator. Naturally, fine speaking skills increase effectiveness of the interpreter, but they are not indispensable. A simple presentation, given with enthusiasm for the subject, is often more lasting than a fluid speech replete with dramatic emphases at selected points.

By all means, an interpreter must be accurate in what he says. I well recall my first campfire program many years ago when serving as a naturalist at Glacier National Park. At the end of the campfire talk I invited questions from the audience, and several were immediately forthcoming. One found me with no ready answer. Not wishing to appear poorly informed, I gave an answer, and immediately wished I could recall it. A gentleman stood up in the crowd and politely, but quite clearly, informed me that I was wrong and proceeded to give the correct answer. To say that my credibility with the crowd suffered would be putting it mildly. To say that my ego suffered would be an understatement. At this point I learned the value of saying "I don't know." If the interpreter cannot be sure of his statements he should not make them in the first place. Certainly he will not lose "face" with the audience by admitting that he does not know the answer; he will be crucified boforo thom comotimo if ho trioc to covor up hic ignoranco with the first glib answer that comes to mind.

An interpreter must know his visitor or audience to be completely successful. All people are different, and have to be treated individually. What is acceptable to one may not be acceptable to another. Some are timid and reserved; others are overbearing and domineering. The same treatment will not work on both. In both cases, tact is essential. If you wear a uniform, some people will show you a deference you do not merit. Others (if you happen to work for a government agency) will let you know in no uncertain terms that you are a servant of the people and that, as taxpayers, they expect special attention! Certainly tact is a real ingredient of the good and successful interpreter!

Many characteristics make up the good interpreter. The above are only a few, but they include the highly essential qualities.

CHAPTER 2

Planning the Interpretive Program

Success or failure of an interpretive program is usually in direct ratio to the amount of thought that has gone into it. Too often an action is taken which seems good at the time, but turns out undesirable from the standpoint of overall interpretive objectives accomplished.

For example, a park was granted funds to build a visitor center, but the money had to be spent immediately. Now there were no plans available to indicate where such a building was to go, how it was to be used, or what was to be in it. In order not to lose the funds, a location was quickly selected, an architect drew up a design, and the building was constructed. Then, and only then, was much thought given to just how the building was to be used. It was most disconcerting for the agency concerned to find that the building was not designed to allow for the type of exhibits needed to tell the area story. Good circulation of visitors within it could not be achieved. Rest rooms were in the wrong location. No provision had been made for audiovisual facilities. The building was so constructed that it could neither be air-conditioned for hot summer months, nor adequately heated in winter. As though all these problems were not enough, there was insufficient outside space for adequate parking. Thus, the value of the building as an interpretive facility was severely reduced. The worst feature, of course, was that it was new and could not be replaced. The area was simply stuck with it for years to come.

All of this adds up to the obvious fact that a well thought out interpretive plan should always be produced for an area before any major steps are taken to put the program into action. This calls for careful study of the entire interpretive operation, and the production of a prospectus.

Just what is an interpretive prospectus? It has been defined as "a preliminary statement that describes an enterprise or program." Stated in a different way, it simply means a "distant view." Basically it is a study document, but *not* necessarily a final plan. It consists of the thinking and planning of the interpreter. It is the blue print of how he believes the total interpretive program for his area should be developed. It may be long or short, depending upon how much he feels should go into it to make his thoughts clear and easily understood. Once completed, it becomes the document upon which all future interpretive development is based.

It should be kept in mind, however, that the finished prospectus presents only the thinking as of the date it is written. It has now reached a "point of departure." It has become subject to improvement in any way possible as soon as it is finally typed. It represents only the basic first step of an ever-developing program, but any changes in the prospectus should be most carefully considered before being made. Change for the sake of change can be damaging. Any interpreter, in studying an existing prospectus, should remember that its proposals are based upon the best thinking and experience of the one who prepared it.

The prospectus is not a complicated document, but should have sufficient detail to be entirely clear to those who may read it. This is essential, for it will be used as a reference by other planners of park or area activities. There is no "best" form in which to prepare it, although the following format has proved to effectively insure comprehensive coverage for the various aspects of the interpretive plan:

INTERPRETIVE PROSPECTUS OUTLINE

1. Interpretive statement defining basic values of the area or subject to be interpreted. These values will determine scope of the plan to be presented.

2. Statement summarizing objectives of the area's interpretive program, defining the major interpretive goals this particular area hopes to accomplish.

3. Factors influencing selection of interpretive means.

    a. The environment.
       (1). Weather and climate.
       (2). Location of the area.
       (3). Geography of the area (if pertinent).

  (4). Natural history values of the area (geology, biology, ecology).

  (5). Historical values of the area.

  (6). Archeological values of the area.

  (7). Other values.

 b. The visitor.

  (1). Origin (his home).

  (2). Type (economic level).

  (3). His background.

   (a). National origin.

   (b). Educational level.

  (4). Visitor use patterns.

  (5). Interpretive activities of other nearby agencies or organizations.

4. The interpretive program.

 a. Present (Describe activities and facilities in some detail)

  (1). Visitor center.

  (2). Wayside exhibits.

  (3). Interpretive signing.

  (4). Self-guiding devices.

  (5). Personal services.

   (a). Conducted walks, hikes and tours.

   (b). On-site assignments.

   (c). Off-site assignments.

   (d). Demonstrations.

   (e). Amphitheater and campfire programs.

  (6). Audiovisual facilities.

  (7). Publications available to visitor.

  (8). Reference library.

  (9). Reference collections.

 b. Proposed facilities and activities (summation of the same items as given above).

  (1). To be developed in some detail, giving thoughts behind each proposal.

 c. Summary chart, showing present and proposed activities and facilities, and locations and manner of treatment of each activity or facility.

5. Content of the proposed program.
   a. The visitor center.
      (1). List what it is to contain and how the building is to function.
      (2). Function of the various rooms.
         (a). Lobby and contents.
         (b). Exhibit room contents. Indicate the stories to be told.
         (c). Audiovisual room.
         (d). Library.
         (e). Work and storage rooms.
         (f). Other (rest rooms, offices, etc.).
   b. Wayside exhibits.
      (1). List locations and basic stories to be covered, and describe how each is to be accomplished.
   c. Interpretive signing.
      (1). List and describe how each is to be accomplished.
   d. Self-guiding devices.
      (1). List and describe what each is to accomplish and how it is to be done.
   e. Personal services.
      (1). Information desk at visitor center or museum.
      (2). Conducted walks.
      (3). Conducted tours (building, archeological site, auto, etc.)
      (4). On-site assignments.
      (5). Off-site assignments.
      (6). Demonstrations.
      (7). Campfire and amphitheater programs.
   f. Audiovisual facilities.
   g. Publications available to the public.
      (1). Folders, maps, etc.
      (2). Publications relating to the area and its features.
      (3). Self-guidance leaflets or booklets.
      (4). Other.
   h. Reference library.
      (1). Contents. General statement.
      (2). How used.
   i. Reference collections.
      (1). List types and scope of collections (biological, geological, historical, archeological, other).

6. **Studies supporting the interpretive program, list of studies made, or being made of value to interpretive plan and program.**

7. **Staffing requirements.**
    a. Present staffing.
    b. Proposed staffing.

8. **Cost estimates for the proposed program. Follow breakdown of facilities and activities as given in item 5 above.**

9. **Map of area showing locations of all present and proposed facilities and activities.**

The prospectus should be developed initially to cover the entire interpretive program for an area, at least in concise outline. It will often be found helpful then to break it down into sections, with each section becoming a detailed statement of how that portion of the prospectus is to be accomplished. Ideally the initial prospectus should be produced 2–3 years ahead of the fiscal year in which implementation is planned. This allows for thorough review by other concerned groups, such as landscape architects, architects, engineers, etc. Some of them will likely be affected, and their needs in turn may require some plan changes.

A sound prospectus is the heart of the interpretive program. Production requires as accurate knowledge of the area, its values, and its potential as is possible to obtain.

echo
ecotype
economic
ecology
ecotone
system
systemic

EcOSyStem

Interpretation through Personal Services

CHAPTER 3

The Problem of Communication

Anyone who has tried to explain something unfamiliar, or give directions how to reach a certain point, knows something about the problem of communication. It is one thing to know yourself what you want to describe, but entirely different when you start to tell someone else about it. Communication is a subject of greatest importance, and something to which the interpreter must give careful consideration. No matter how much he knows about his subject, if he cannot transmit this knowledge to his listener, he has failed.

Many ideas are advanced today on the best way to communicate with another person. Some, however, are basic, and hold the key to understanding by your listener. Let us look at them:

A really big problem is putting into simple language what is being said. This is not as easy as it sounds. Each of us talks from his own frame of reference. The interpreter whose background is biology, or perhaps geology, will be familiar with certain terms and ideas not common to his listener. When he talks about an ecosystem, he may well be leaving his listener far behind. While the latter is trying hard to grasp the meaning of the word, other thoughts being expressed are barely registered, if at all. I once heard a speaker give a talk on geology that was most interesting to anyone familiar with the subject. However, his audience left in a much bewildered frame of mind, simply because they could not understand what he was saying. He talked about faults, thrusts, isostatic conditions, tectonics, Permian and Cretaceous time, and used other terms equally unfamiliar to the listeners. He spoke for the professional geologist, not for the public, failing to grasp the fact that one must gauge the likely background and experience of the audience in selecting words to describe the subject. While he made the common mistake of using technical terms for a non-technical audience, we do not mean that technical terms should never be used. Rather, they should be used sparingly, and explained when first used, just to make sure listeners understand. Keep the talk or conversation simple. Don't "talk down" to the audience, but keep the talk on an understandable level. Some speakers go too far in the direction of simplicity and act as though the listeners are no better informed than a child. Nothing can terminate communication more quickly!

Often we use words that have more than one common meaning, thus failing to put across the true significance and value of what we are trying to say. The common word "frog" may mean different things to members of an audience. To some it means an amphibian; to some it means part of a horse's hoof; to others the place where two railroad irons are joined; to some an aid in arranging flowers; and to still others, it might even mean a Frenchman, or a five dollar bill! The word "fast" is another example of how a simple word may convey the wrong idea. It may mean: speed; being tied to something; a color that will not run; doing without food for a time; or, a free-swinging socialite. Much depends upon the listener's background as to the image a word will bring to mind. Certainly all terms used should be carefully chosen for clarity.

Rate of speaking is very important. Many people are not trained to hear rapid conversation, and cannot grasp ideas poured out too rapidly. One must learn to speak at a moderate rate, and at the same time, speak clearly and enunciate distinctly. Speaking too slowly is as deadly as a machine-gun type of delivery. There is nothing much more boring and sleep producing to an audience than to have the speaker drag out his words and phrases in a slow, measured way. So vary the speed of your presentation to add emphasis to important points.

Stay away from slang. It is true there are some expressions that seem to describe things better than more accepted forms of speech. However, there is real danger that the slang word selected may not mean to the listener what it means to you. It may have overtones to him that he will not accept. He may also resent slang terms simply because he does not agree with the use of such.

Another "don't" concerns references to states, especially when used as the subject of a wise crack, an uncomplimentary reference, or an object of ridicule. There is always the probability that someone in the audience will be from the state mentioned, and is proud of it. If so, you can be sure he will resent your reference and will have a mental block against what you are trying to tell him.

We must also remember that some things we say are relative in their meanings and really do not tell the listener anything. For example, a wife calls her husband and says that dinner is served. He calls back and says "I'll be there in a minute." He didn't actually mean that he would be there in that time; simply that he couldn't be there immediately, and that some time would elapse before he reached the dining table. Speakers and others in the interpretive field often resort to this sort of vagueness in describing something. We hear such expressions as: "quite some time elapsed," "it is only a short distance," or possibly "it is a relatively soft rock." None of these mean much to anyone except the person who said them.

Simple illustrations are most useful. If possible, choose those reflecting in some degree the listener's experience and background. If speaking to a group of farmers, one would normally not use illustrations taken from a chemistry laboratory.

A good interpreter is always keenly aware of the fact that listening is a skill few people possess. Most people *hear* what is being said, but only a small percentage really *listen*. Herein lies the difference between success and failure for most communicators. Only when a person really listens has he some chance of understanding what you are trying to tell him. If he has not been trained to listen, he is likely to grasp only a part of what you are saying. The relationship between what you tell a person and what he actually retains can easily be shown by the following simple diagram: (read from bottom up)

What he remembered about the subject later
What he retained about the subject initially
What he understood about what you said
What he actually listened to about the subject
What he heard about the subject
What you actually told him about the subject
What you think you told him about the subject
What you know about the subject

It becomes quite apparent that much of what we have to say will be wasted effort, even if your audience listens carefully. Keep in mind that the normal person retains only about 10% of what you tell him, if he actually tries to absorb your message. The lesson is obvious: Don't overload the listener or audience with a vast assortment of data. Choose a limited number of key ideas that you want to present, and make these clear.

Several important points should be considered when we try to communicate. All are of value and are not listed in order of priority:

A person's response to what you tell him depends in large measure how he reacts to your word selection, tone of voice, actions, attitudes, mood, personality and appearance. Failure in any one of these categories may mean a decided lessening of acceptance.

A person reacts to you in terms of his own attitudes, moods, character, knowledge of the subject, need for importance and social status. Your background and experience may differ widely from his. He may have come from a poor family, while you did not. He may not have much education, while you may be a college graduate. There are so many ways in which the two of you differ. Consider what sort of problem faces you in presenting a talk to a large audience. Somehow you must present an image that everyone will be likely to accept.

You may fail to convey the information he needs and can understand. As an example, try giving a person directions about how to get to some specific point. Loss of communication frequently follows.

His beliefs influence what he hears; he will have prejudices that may govern his thinking. As an example, it may be quite difficult to convince your listener that a snake has value, even in nature.

His emotional state of mind will in large measure control what he hears. If he has just had a difference of opinion with someone, he may not be too receptive to what you say.

He may be fearful about what you are saying and not get the message. For example, telling him it is perfectly safe to travel alone through wilderness country may not be accepted. Your message about the wonders of such a trip simply will not be received.

He may suspect your motives and think you are trying to trick him into something. He may feel that what you say and what you mean are two different things.

He may fail to evaluate what you are saying and the meaning may elude him.

He may simply not believe you. This can happen with any subject you bring up. If what you say doesn't sound true, based upon his knowledge and experience, he may simply refuse to accept your statements.

Good communication depends upon feedback. How many questions does your hearer ask? Possibly you have made your message so clear that he hasn't a single question to ask, but such isn't likely.

Courtesy, consideration and tact are vital if he is to be in a receptive frame of mind. The desire to hear and understand must be there before he will really listen to your message.

Communication enters interpretation in many forms. It is essential in public contact, talks, guided activities, signs, exhibits, audiovisual materials, publications, etc. All will be discussed in the pages that follow.

CHAPTER 4

Illustrated and Non-illustrated Talks

You have just attended a campfire talk, and something about it simply did not stir your enthusiasm. The speaker appeared to know his subject, but still the whole program seemed flat. The period before the talk started was tiresome, and the person who served as master of ceremonies was rather ordinary. He had tried to inject some pep into the crowd by leading the group in song, but wasn't too good at it and they didn't seem to respond. Still he had tried. His announcements had been pretty lengthy. They took up a lot of time and left you wondering when he was going to present the speaker of the evening. Finally, the speaker was introduced, and the program moved along for another hour. You had a sense of relief when it finally ended, and you could stand up and move around.

What was wrong with the talk? Perhaps nothing on which you could really lay your hands. To the trained interpreter, however, many things were obviously wrong. The chances were that the speaker hadn't done his "home work" before the program. He had failed to observe several of the little things during his talk that should not have happened. Also, the MC was definitely a part of the problem.

Planning and presenting a talk, whether at an evening campfire program in the out-of-doors, inside a big auditorium, or during a demonstration is not a simple thing. It calls for more than just the ability to stand before a group and talk. As one of the most important functions in any interpretive program, contributing largely to success or failure, it deserves most careful review. Let us examine the various elements involved.

A campfire or amphitheater program, using color slides or film, calls for a bit more thought and preparation than one given in an auditorium. So many more things can happen out-doors than inside.

In either case, the speaker and MC should arrive at least 30 minutes before program time. This allows time to greet the people as they arrive and to:

Check all equipment in advance. Do this carefully, as a breakdown in the middle of a talk due to carelessness is inexcusable.

Be sure all projector lenses are clean. Projected in large screen size, lint and dirt of any type are very distracting.

Be sure sufficient projection bulbs are on hand to replace any that may burn out. Each bulb should be replaced shortly after its guaranteed life has been reached, and a record of projection time for the bulb should be kept with the projector. This almost insures there will be no burn outs during the course of a talk. Don't gamble with old bulbs, even though they still burn.

Always check extension cords and plugs to see that all are in good shape.

Check the screen for dirt, spots, etc. If a roll-up type, check for dead moths that may have been trapped the last time the screen was used.

Be sure the projector is correctly pre-focused and that the picture does not "bleed" off the screen. With automatic focus on most still projectors, this is all that will be necessary to insure sharp pictures through the talk.

Be sure that pointers, light arrows, etc., are in place (if the speaker plans to use such). The best pointer has a flourescent tip which glows when the projection light hits it. Flashlights with light arrows are easily made or can be purchased.

If a campfire is a part of the program, be sure the fire dies down before the projection portion begins. This will help insure a bright picture image on the screen.

Many campfire and amphitheater programs are preceded by music. If music is used, be sure the selection is appropriate and designed to harmonize with the theme of the talk to follow. One wouldn't use stirring marches to introduce a talk on flowers!

Let us now look at the MC. His job is very important. If he does it well the speaker will receive a relaxed, friendly audience, and a lot of problems he might face will likely never arise. If he fails the speaker may be faced with an audience having a "make me interested" attitude.

When program time arrives, the MC takes over the stage. A number of things should be considered regarding this part of the operation.

The speaker (interpreter) who is to give the talk should wait off stage, and keep watch to see that all is going as planned. For example, if a campfire is being used, it is usually a foregone conclusion that someone will appoint himself to the job of feeding the fire. The speaker should watch this to see that a bonfire isn't blazing at projection time.

The MC should introduce himself, but in a simple way. No long sounding titles and experience backgrounds are necessary. He should be friendly, enthusiastic (but not too bubbly), and obviously hoping the audience is enjoying itself.

He can use a number of "ice breaker" devices to get the crowd into a good mood, but these should not use too much time. He must remember the old adage that "the mind can absorb as long as the seat can stand!" There is a talk yet to be given, and seats tend to become hard!

After the "ice breaker" can come singing. By all means the MC should be able to carry a tune if he is going to lead. Too often an MC is put in front of an audience to lead singing when he simply cannot do it. The crowd may be sympathetic toward him, but he has definitely lost them when they feel sorry for him. If your MC cannot do this job reasonably well, don't have him try! Better no songs at all than a dismal failure! Use familiar songs—not the latest hit parade selections. The old favorites are always good, and it is often surprising how many in the audience will know them.

This is the time for any "action songs" by the audience. It also gives the children a chance to work off some energy before the talk begins, and they are likely to be a bit quieter at that time. Action songs should come early in the singing program, with more relaxing ones used later to settle the crowd. The MC certainly doesn't want to turn over a foot-stamping, hand-clapping crowd to the speaker! Programs given in an auditorium are more formal than those in the out-of-doors, so singing may not be chosen.

Any announcements of the next day's interpretive events, etc., can be given after the singing.

The MC should make the introduction of the speaker short and to the point, announce his subject for him, and be ready to help in any way possible as the speaker does his job.

So much for the MC. Various persons have various approaches, but the duties discussed above are basic.

As would be supposed, the speaker should have several things in mind as he prepares and presents his part of the program. Suppose you are going to talk. Here are a number of points you should consider:

First decide what sort of message you wish to present. There should be a theme to your subject. This will allow for good organization of subject material. A good title is important, especially if thought provoking and not too involved.

Develop a talk that can be illustrated; not illustrations that are looking for a talk! What often happens is that a speaker will decide he will cover, let us say, the subject of mammals. So he goes to the slide cabinet and picks out all the slides on mammals he can find. Then he arranges them in some sort of order, and decides what he is going to say about them. Actually the process should be reversed. He should first decide what he wants to say about mammals, and then choose slides to illustrate the points he wishes to bring out.

Choose slides as background, illustrative material and not something that must be explained. If a scene or slide chosen must be explained before it is understandable, it is a poor choice. There are, of course, some exceptions to this rule, as you may wish to use charts, etc., which need some interpretation.

Be sure the slides chosen portray the mood you wish to develop.

Choose only good color shots, and not a wide range of color

values. It is very poor technique to show the viewer a series of good color scenes, and then suddenly confront him with a slide of poor quality. The difference is too obvious, and he will certainly not be too complimentary in his thoughts at that moment. Try to retain approximately the same color density for all slides chosen. Light color to dark color and back to light is a bit disconcerting.

Select slides that are properly framed. How often have you seen pictures projected where the slide frame has slipped, showing a white area or something equally disturbing? Check all bindings for possible slippage if the slide is mounted in glass.

Don't use a slide you will have to apologize for. Choose film that is in good condition.

Don't use large numbers of slides. This is not a "slow motion" movie, or as one naturalist once expressed it, "galloping postcards!" Neither should there be too few, requiring some to be on the screen too long.

Have at least one key thing in mind that the chosen slide will illustrate.

If maps or charts are used, be sure they are sharp and the color is used judiciously. Too many colors on the same map or chart are confusing. Be sure, also, that the map will project large enough for everyone to see its details.

Don't expect the slides to carry the talk. This is not a travelogue such as one can use after a summer's vacation trip.

The talk should last not more than 35–40 minutes, so select numbers of slides accordingly. Keep in mind that you will want to close out the talk when the audience wishes you had gone ahead —not after they start wondering when you will quit!

If possible, use a viewing table for the final layout. As a final precaution, be sure all slides are free of dirt and dust.

Some speakers prepare a talk in outline form before trying to fit the slides into place. This is usually quite helpful. Some actually write out the talk beforehand. This is time consuming, but many speakers find it essential.

With the talk now planned and organized, you can turn your

attention to the actual presentation. In general, you should divide the talk into four basic elements:

Strike a spark with the opening sentence. You may have a blase audience, and must try to get attention at once. They aren't likely to be all ears and eyes, just waiting for your message. Possibly they may even have a bored attitude; some persons may be a bit sleepy, especially those who have been traveling. An opening remark of "One of the problems in the National Parks today is that of preserving the Giant Sequoias" sounds all right, but people will likely sit up and take notice is you say "We are about to love the sequoias to death!" There is the classic story of the visiting minister in a small country church with a sleepy audience and a hot morning. He opened his sermon with the observation that "this is a damned hot morning—at least that is what I heard a man say outside a few minutes ago!"

To have real meaning for the listener, the subject must in some way touch him or his experience. It is difficult to take facts, no matter how interesting they may seem to you, and make your listener react to them unless you tie them to his personal interests.

Don't take too long to get at the meat of the subject. Some speakers try to say the same thing over and over again in a different way. They ramble. By all means stick to your theme, as this is the message you are trying to get across. Don't get all involved in your subject and try to tell everything you know about it. Select the most important aspects of it, and restrict your comments to them. Use examples that are to the point, but use some. The phrases "for example" or "for instance" are attention getters. Be judicious about the use of jokes. Don't fill up your talk with jokes that are obviously planted. The listener likes to laugh, but he likes to hear something of interest, also. Jokes should be used to highlight or explain some point you wish to make—not merely to get laughs. Be sure the jokes you use will not offend anyone.

Encourage some sort of action. What do you want the listener to do? This is the whole point of your presentation. This is the place for your punch thought. If you want him to look, see, visit, explore, experience, preserve, conserve, study—this is the time to emphasize such.

The actual presentation of your talk involves so many things that one could fill a book with them. Whole courses are given on the art of public speaking, so no attempt will be made here to compete with them. However, there are a number of things that should be stressed:

Have a friendly introduction. Make your audience feel that you appreciate their being at your program. Watch your location on stage. This is especially important if you are using a microphone, as there may be a feedback from the speakers if you are not positioned properly. A necklace type microphone, or one that transmits, is by far the best to use, as it allows freedom of action on your part.

If using slides, stand well to one side of the screen. This is so you will not block the view of anyone. Keep in mind that those sitting down in front and to one side have difficulty seeing the screen unless you are well out of the line of vision.

Avoid references to the slides, unless there is something you want to be sure the viewer sees. Too many speakers have the very bad habit of saying "Here we see . . ." or "This slide shows . . ." or some such statement when the slide comes on the screen. You should have your talk so well in mind that you could go on without slides if the projector should happen to fail. The slides are merely background material for the things you are saying.

Use a pointer to indicate any object on the screen. Do not try to describe its location. When using the pointer, don't "stab," but move it fluidly. Be on the side of the screen best suited for use of the pointer. A right-handed person should not be standing on the left side of the screen, and vice versa. Signal for your next slide a second or two before actually needed. If you wait until you have completed your thoughts on the previous one, there is apt to be an awkward pause before the next slide appears.

Slides should normally not stay on the screen *longer* than 20–30 seconds before changing. There may be occasions when you will need one longer. If possible, remedy this by adding a second slide on the same subject.

Carefully pronounce words that are sometimes difficult to hear clearly or to grasp.

Use familiar examples to put across a point, even homely ones.

Keep the language simple; don't get academic or involved.

Leave the dramatics to professional actors. Some drama may safely be injected into the talk, but care should be exercised.

Be courteous in what you say. By all means, do not make wise cracks about persons.

Be enthusiastic, but not bombastic, and by all means don't be an obvious "know it all."

Likely there will be times when you will need to give a different kind of illustrated talk, such as one in which you use hand-held objects. Various types of situations arise where this may happen. For example:

An object is brought to you. This necessitates an impromptu talk to properly interpret the object.

You may want to talk about objects you discover on a guided walk.

You may have an "on-site" assignment where an object or objects can be used to tell visitors about the feature.

You may wish to demonstrate how something works.

You may want to give a formal talk before an audience using hand-held materials. This type of presentation is commonly considered one of our most helpful means of communication with groups. It is also quite often the least understood in terms of how best to accomplish.

In planning such a talk, whether before a formal audience or an informal trail group, there are a number of things to consider:

Choose a subject for your talk that can be shown.

If possible, choose a subject that may fall within the experience of the visitor.

Organize the material to be shown in logical sequence. This will make it much easier for your listener to grasp.

Outline the talk visually, otherwise you will likely miss several important points. There will not be slides available to help you remember.

Keep your presentation somewhat in story form.

In giving a talk using hand-held objects, several factors should be considered:

Be sure the background is suitable. Check the objects to be shown for color and shape. The background should be contrasting, if possible.

Lay out all objects in order of sequence for showing. This enables you to keep your mind on what you are saying.

Hold each object steady as you speak. It is difficult for viewers to see detail of a moving object.

Turn the object slowly, if necessary to change its position. This allows visual relationships to be grasped by the viewers.

If shown at night, good light on the object is a necessity. Without good lighting any details you wish to show cannot be seen. You can, however, use a hand specimen of some type as an "attention getter." The audience will listen intently to what you are saying in order to find out what is in your hand and what you intend to say about it.

If on trail, at demonstrations, etc., let the visitor examine the object being shown, if practicable.

Take care in handling live objects. Visitors can get disturbed if your live object should happen to be a reptile.

Handle potentially unsafe objects yourself. Normally you should not use them, but if you should need to do so, do not let the visitors handle them.

Watch the object part of the time as you show it, thus focusing attention.

Slowly point out features of the object. If before a seated audience, use a pointer if one is available.

If the object has a use, show what it is or pantomime the use.

Appeal to the viewer's imagination where possible.

Be sure that any children present can see what is being shown. Too often we gear presentations only for older people.

It may be that you are not using slides or other materials in your talk. Perhaps it is not illustrated in any manner. If so, in addition to the points that pertain to illustrated talks, the following should be considered:

Always face the audience. Your voice will not reach many if you speak across stage. While this is no problem when using a microphone, it is vital when you depend entirely on your voice for audience contact.

Speak at a slower speed than you would normally use indoors, if your program is being given outside. It is more difficult to project your voice out-of-doors, and words tend to blur.

Don't speak in short phrases. They make your presentation jerky, and, as a result, distracting.

Always remember that what you are saying is familiar to you, but likely not to the listener, and you cannot show him.

Stick to a "story" approach. It is difficult to carry the audience over distractions that may arise. When these occur, people may not connect what you have said with what you are saying unless the tie-up is easy to grasp.

Use some gestures. They can be seen even by the light of a campfire. If you don't, you will appear too stiff

Have a place for your hands. This seems one of the biggest problems to most speakers. Putting them into a trousers pocket isn't the answer either!

Don't slouch or lean on a podium. Stand reasonably upright. Be relaxed, but not too casual.

Don't walk around too much. Pacing the floor like a caged lion is definitely distracting.

Watch the audience as you talk. Don't watch something about the 10th limb up in a tree, or on the ceiling of the auditorium. Some speakers find it difficult to look into the faces of the audience. They say they are nervous enough just giving the talk, let alone having to watch faces out front. Yet, each person in the audience likes to feel that you are talking directly to him. Try this. Simply look over the crowd when you come on stage (or before) and select four or five persons in various parts of the audience who seem to have friendly faces. Then talk to those people in a conversational way, and nervousness tends to quickly disappear. As you turn your gaze from one of your chosen people to another, the audience will feel that you are looking at them individually and not at one certain person.

If at a campfire, don't have the fire too high. Not only does it distract, but it may become too hot for those persons seated nearby.

If at a campfire, don't add fuel during the talk. It breaks the thought you are developing. If fuel must be added, have someone else chosen in advance to do this job.

In closing your talk, here are points to remember:

When you come to the end of the talk, bring it to a close. Don't draw it out and let it drag. Anything said after the message has been brought out is anticlimax.

Close out with a "punch" thought, if possible.

Close out "on time." Many people have allotted a specific amount of time to hear your talk. If you advertise the program to last an hour, limit it to that. Children are often brought to evening programs and the parents want to get them home and into bed.

Invite questions upon completion of the talk. Several persons will probably want additional information.

Be courteous in answering questions. This may be the only opportunity for some of the audience to talk to you, especially if you are in uniform. Some people are a bit reserved when talking to a uniformed person for the first time.

Don't obviously want to leave as soon as the program is over. If you are in *too* much of a hurry, you have the wrong job! Never let haste cause failure to be friendly.

There are, of course, several devices that can go far toward making any talk more interesting. One of the most effective is the use of fluorescent light and fluorescent chalk. All that is needed is an easel set up on stage near the screen, with the light mounted on its top, a pad of plain paper and a number of different colored chalks. The light can be turned on at any time during the talk, as it is only faintly visible to the audience. If you wish to draw a chart or perhaps sketch something to supplement what you have on the screen, you can do so in any combination of colors. Under the fluorescent light the chalk glows in the darkness, appearing like so much magic on the paper pad. Also the entire drawing can be done prior to the start of the program and the light turned on when needed. This device in no way impairs the slide projection, and can be used to enhance the quality of your presentation.

An aid that should be considered when developing campfire talks, or other talks where electricity is not available, is the portable sound system. Several battery powered types are available at reasonable cost.

How do you determine when a talk is well presented? There are a number of ways in which a speaker's performance can be checked. A rather complete critique was developed at the Mather Training Center (a National Park Service facility where training is given in interpretive skills) and is quite helpful in evaluating either an illustrated or non-illustrated talk. This sheet follows:

Speaker's Attitudes	Points	Comments
1. Enthusiastic?		
2. Confident?		
3. Courteous?		
4. Friendly?		
5. Relaxed?		

Overall impression of the talk by the Evaluator, Total Points Scored _____.

Point Scores:

    0– 20 –Weak
    21– 40 –Fair
    41– 60 –Average
    61– 80 –Very good
    81–100 –Outstanding

Additional points for consideration, if talk is illustrated by color slides (Same grade scale as for above):

1. Color quality?   _____
2. Composition of slide?   _____
3. Position on screen?   _____
4. Condition of slides?   _____
5. Quantity of slides?   _____
6. Slides used effectively? _____

0– 3 –Weak
4– 9 –Fair
10–15 –Average
16–20 –Very good
21–24 –Outstanding

General Comments:

_____

_____

_____

_____

_____

_____

_____

_____

_____

_____

_____

_____

_____

_____

_____

_____

_____

_____

Top-Bryce Canyon National Park. Left-Discovery hike, finding thousands of ladybugs. Right-Winter tour, Crater Lake National Park. (photo by Richard M. Brown)

CHAPTER 5

Guided Walks and Tours

The guided tour, whether a guided walk, a caravan tour or one taken over snow-covered slopes on skis, is without doubt the most enjoyable interpretive activity an area can offer. It has a special value in that it is usually thoroughly enjoyed by both the visitor and the tour leader. Sometimes an interpretive activity, especially a daily one, can become somewhat of a chore. As days pass, the task may become a routine affair, with the interpreter looking forward to the end of such an arrangement rather than anticipating its beginning. However, such is normally not true of the guided tour. Here the leader can be sure he will not have the same events taking place over and over again every time he goes out, unless he wishes it to be so. New things constantly come to his attention, especially if his guided walk takes him into the field of natural history. Here anything can happen, and often does. The guided walk can well be the peak experience for the visitor in any area, allowing him to see and do something he would otherwise miss. In the out-of-doors he can experience the use of his several senses, something he seldom finds happening in the home environment. A walk has a touch of exploration, of becoming acquainted with things many people never experience. Natural history, history, archeology, environment, ecology—all open new doors of interest to him. In no other interpretive activity is there a greater variety of opportunities for the trip leader to enrich the visitor's experience.

TYPES OF GUIDED WALKS OR TOURS

Guided walks break down into three main categories: the nature walk; the historic house, grounds or building walk; and the archeology walk. Each has its own characteristics and values, with some features common to all.

There must be an objective, if the walk is to be successful. There must be some organization if it doesn't become a mixture of odds and ends of apparently unrelated values. Each walk should have some reason for being, something to contribute to visitor enjoyment and understanding. Some thought or concept must be presented for consideration. Those who go along are likely to know little, or perhaps nothing, of what you are going to tell or show. The possibilities are almost limitless as you contemplate what can be done to enhance their understanding of what they see.

Various types of nature talks have been tried, all successful in varying degrees. Some most often used are:

1. The general nature walk.

This is a "discovery" type, in which the leader simply takes his group along a route that is determined as he goes. He has a spot where he expects to terminate the walk, but usually no pre-determined plan as to just how he will reach it. Everything seen along the way becomes a potential source of interest. It may be a tree, flower, rock, bird, mammal, insect or whatever is to be found. Everyone is encouraged to look for anything that may interest him, and, once found, the leader discusses it with the group. It is a real challenge to the leader, in that many things may be found about which he knows very little.

This type of walk has many fine features, likely the most important of which is that each member of the group can be an active participant. The walk becomes *his* walk, not just one the leader has dreamed up. It introduces the various group members to new and heretofore unknown natural history subjects, and is an almost perfect lead into understanding the ecological environment.

It does have its weaknesses. Many persons are reluctant to leave an established path or trail. This is especially true in a forested situation, where the unknown may seem to present a threat to persons unfamiliar with such an environment. This is very noticeable among adults who have small children along. There is always the possibility that some less agile person in the group will injure himself.

2. The thematic nature walk.

This is the walk most often used, and is designed to reveal to the group a coordinated concept, natural relationship or similar subject. The leader tries to show how and why something happens in the natural scene. He may wish to demonstrate forest ecology, the influence of man on the forest community, the way in which natural forces are operating, or perhaps the story of a single species of tree, such as the sequoia. The possible list is broad indeed.Such a walk is almost always taken along a pre-determined route which lends itself to development of the chosen theme. The leader knows in advance where he will make stops. This does not mean there will not be unscheduled stops along the way; after all, a bear or some other creature may cross the trail and become the center of attention for several minutes. However, interruptions do not change the basic theme and the leader simply returns to the story he was developing when the interruption occurred.

Its greatest strength lies in the story or thematic approach. It is easy to tie its many facets together in the visitor's mind into a well coordinated whole that will be easy to remember. It is a "safe" type of walk, and seldom does any visitor feel uncertain about venturing along. Most people can "come as you are" without need for any special gear, so the leader can take his group to places many would never venture out to see by themselves.

Its weaknesses are also apparent. This walk tends to lack the individual participation that characterizes "discovery" type walks. There is a tendency for the group to be made up of two units: the leader, and the rest of the party. The leader "tells," the group "listens." Basically there is real danger such a walk becomes the leader's and not the group's. A careful choice of guiding methods used will eliminate this problem. Much depends upon the resourcefulness and experience of the leader.

3. The special walk.

This might be called a "quality" type walk. Many people are interested in special natural history subjects.

Among the most popular of these is the bird walk. The makeup of this group will be varied. There will likely be serious bird students along, as well as a goodly number of people who won't know one bird from another, but who would like to know more. The leader must be reasonably well versed in bird life of the region, not only in the appearance and habits of the bird likely to be seen, but also its call notes and songs. The walk will almost always leave the established trail or pathway. It usually calls for durable clothing and footwear, plus binoculars, if available. It has much in common with the discovery walk, in that its stops are unscheduled and the route may be changed as the walk develops. It is not likely, however, to have people along who are timid about leaving an established trail.

This walk enables you, as its leader, to disclose a whole new world of interest for many people, an interest that can be transferred to where they live, with long time activity a likely prospect. An aid to this type of walk is the small cassette tape recorder, with a cartridge of recorded bird songs and calls of the species most likely to be seen.

The flower walk is another popular one. It can often be accomplished along an established trail. In fact, there is real danger to the plants if the group is allowed to wander into the flower fields. This type of trip is a special favorite among the women visitors, and you should not be surprised to find that men will be in a decided minority in almost any group. Here again, you as the leader will need to know more than just the basic information about each flower species seen. Interesting ecological problems faced by the plant and how it solves them are always well received.

Leading this type of walk is relatively easy, as such a group is normally anxious to see and hear, but not disturb or destroy. I recall one incident, however, where a young naturalist led such a group along a trail through a flower-covered slope. Among other things, he carefully explained the urge sometimes experienced to pick a handful of the colorful creations. About the time he finished, a lady came up to him with a large bunch of flowers in her hand and asked: "Ranger, what kind of flowers are these?" To which the young naturalist (who lost all of his tact and patience at the same time) replied: "Lady, those are *picked* flowers!"

The forest walk is another that can usually be accomplished along an established trail. Its operation and characteristics are not much different from those discussed above.

The geology walk is quite similar in its treatment to those above, with exception of the guided cave tour.

The latter is carried on in an entirely different environment from other special walks. It requires careful consideration of the group's comfort, as they may be exposed to moisture, chill, and narrow passageways where one's vision is often impaired and a bumped head is commonly experienced. This is another situation where some of your group may feel a bit insecure as they go underground. You must always be prepared for the possibility of electric failure in the cave lights (if so illuminated). The group must be conditioned in advance of the tour that such might conceivably happen, and what should be done if it occurs. Safety thus becomes a major concern to the leader.

The history walk or tour is usually more concise in its planning. Here, you deal normally with fixed objects, or take the party through an area where history was once made. Most of what is shown must be explained. The group is most unlikely to have much background knowledge of the story to be told, although history buffs are frequently members of the tour. You usually have a wide variety of events that you can relate to keep the walk from becoming a simple routine job.

The archeology walk is very similar in planning to the history tour. The story of early man and his activities is a favorite subject with many visitors, and a well thought out tour is a real crowd pleaser. Here again the leader must do most of the explaining, as group background is normally quite limited.

GUIDANCE METHODS

Techniques found effective in leading walks are many and varied. Usually the technique used by the leader is one with which he feels secure. Success depends on his individual skill. Most leaders use one of four methods, or a combination of them. Let us consider each in detail, examining both strengths and weaknesses.

1. Telling

This is the most commonly used of all guided tour methods. Here the leader simply takes his party along a pre-determined route, and usually stops at pre-determined points. At each point of interest, he has carefully assembled in his mind an array of information about the story to be told, and relates this to the assembled group before going on to the next stop. There is normally little group involvement. The leader tells—the group listens. The leader may invite questions before proceeding to the next stop, but even these afford only brief breaks in the time schedule. This method gives the leader complete control of the group, and enables him to keep all the subject material pertinent to the tour. The technique is very popular with tour leaders, especially on history and archeology walks, and also shows up on the nature walks.

If the tour leader has a reasonably good personality, a good speaking voice, and a comprehensive knowledge of his subject, this system is almost always a success. People will leave feeling pretty well pleased with having gone along.

There is a basic weakness in the method. It definitely divides the group into two units—the leader, and the party. The tour is basically his; the group is along to listen and absorb what is being said. There tends to be a lack of group unity. Individuals may relate to the leader, but not so much with each other. The field of interest of each visitor tends to be sharply reduced to conform to that of the leader, with little opportunity to broaden the scope of the subject being presented.

2. Telling and Showing

This is also a popular method with many tour leaders. Basically it is the "telling" with interesting demonstrations added to lend strength to the presentation. A good demonstration is almost certain to be well received, and a number scattered through a guided walk will insure an appreciative audience. Here some individual participation can be utilized, as members of the tour can often be used in the demonstration. "Living history" tours can use this method to advantage. I recall one instance where an old Civil War cannon was the center of attraction. The tour leader asked a number of children about 10–11 years of age to assist him in explaining how the cannon was loaded and fired. Naturally the children were quite ready to do a bit of play acting, so he had no trouble in choosing a "gun crew" from eager volunteers. As he explained to the audience the duties of each member of a gun crew, he assigned a youngster to play that part. When all was ready, he had the "gun crew" go through the motions of "loading" the cannon and finally "firing" it. The whole affair was a rousing success, the audience grasped the story being told, and the children got to play make-believe with an interesting object. Parents of the children involved were pleased their youngsters got to take part. The leader's rapport with the group couldn't have been better.

3. Drawing Out

There is little doubt that this is one of the most effective methods available to a leader. There is also no doubt that it requires him to be more alert and knowledgeable. At the same time, it tends to make him less sure of his ground.

You, as the leader, can choose a wide variety of approaches. If on a nature walk, you can let discovery be the primary focus, you can mix in a thematic approach, or you can include contributions of all kinds. In this method you encourage members of the group to find those things that are of interest to them. One may want to learn more about the ecology of a rotten log; another may wonder about how a bird lives; and another may be interested in some facet of history or early day Indian life. In each instance the leader pursues the subject in some detail, but instead of simply telling the interested person and the group what he knows about it, he draws the answers from the group. This is done by asking questions, the answers to which will throw light on the subject. Here is where the simple, but sage, advice attributed to Kipling is worth remembering:

"I have six faithful working men who help in all I do. Their names are why, what, when, where, how and who."

Ask such questions as: "What is it doing here?" or "how does nature use it?" or "how might man have used it?" or "why is it found here and not somewhere else?" The object, of course, is to start the group to thinking, and someone almost certainly will come up with an answer that will open still more doors for additional questions. Through this questioning method, the important things known about the subject can be brought out. Occasionally you, as the leader, will have to fill in with information that no one in the group is likely to know. You may also have to ask an occasional "leading question" to keep things moving. In the end you have had a very interested group that has worked out its own answers under your direction.

There are real strengths in this method. Basically the walk becomes the group's and not yours. You are still the leader, but you now have a different function. You lead in thought, but the group furnishes most of the information needed. This, in itself, is almost certain to insure success for the walk. Each visitor enjoys getting involved, especially when he knows something about the subject that he can contribute. Every person has an ego, large or small, which he enjoys exercising upon occasion. This method allows him to pamper it a bit!

There are also weaknesses to be considered. The method is time consuming, so the leader must be alert to this fact. Seldom can he set a distance objective and make it as he has planned—if he allows the group to really get involved in the discussion. There is a possibility that someone in the group will try to dominate the trip, but this can happen on any type of tour. Also, some member of the tour may, and often does, come up with the wrong answer, and you, as the leader, must tactfully "rescue" him. If you are really resourceful, you will endeavor to fit his answer into the discussion at a later point.

4. Telling, Showing and Drawing Out.

This obviously combines the three previous methods. It is also the one this writer feels is the most effective of the four. It allows you, the leader, to tell when it is best to do so, demonstrate where you wish, and draw the group into the discussion at any time desired. It allows complete control over the speed at which the tour moves. It allows you to operate on a time schedule, reach a field or building tour objective as planned, and present a well balanced program to everyone.

I see no real weaknesses in this method. It does require a well informed, interested and alert leader to do it well. It is virtually guaranteed to eliminate the "routine" tour. It is definitely stimulating to you and to your group.

OPERATING THE GUIDED WALK OR TOUR

Leading a group of people along a trail, into a natural area, through an historic house or area, or around an archeological site is not difficult, but there is an amazing number of "dos" and "don'ts" to remember if the walk is to be most effectively led. Even the skillful leader will definitely weaken his performance if he overlooks any of these items:

1. Pre-walk activities.

Select a place to meet the group that will be pleasant to those having to wait for the tour to begin. Many persons arrive early for a walk. If you have chosen a bright, sunny place to meet, and the day happens to be a bit on the hot side, members of your group may not be in too good a frame of mind by the time the tour starts. If there is a place where they can sit down, so much the better. If a beautiful view is to be had, still better.

A routed or lettered sign at the meeting place listing time of departure, and days on which the walk is given, is helpful. This is especially true where several guided walks originate at the same point every day. Many visitors try to operate on a time schedule, and information of assistance in planning their activities is useful.

Be sure you have any special equipment along that will be needed, such as binoculars, light meter, etc. If a nature walk, the binoculars are most appropriate. A light meter to help those taking color stills or movies is much appreciated.

Always arrive at the meeting place well in advance of departure time. Remain there and don't wander around, as you will only confuse visitors planning to take the walk. When people arrive at the meeting place they expect to see the person there who will lead the tour. If you do not stay at this location, many may be uncertain as to whether they are at the correct place.

As people arrive, greet them cordially. Don't just let them stand around. A friendly reception helps put them at ease, and is the first step in welding them into a cohesive group.

Engage early comers in conversation, if possible. Don't be "pushy," but get them started talking. It helps make them a part of the group, and puts you on good terms with them before the walk begins. This also helps to get each person acquainted with others on the tour.

By all means, plan to start the walk on schedule. Don't just wait around for possible late comers. Visitors who arrived on time have made an effort to do so, and should not have to wait for less punctual persons.

2. Before the tour leaves.

Introduce yourself before starting the walk. This is not simply a matter of ego; the group will want to know who you are. Make the introduction simple for the group will not be interested in a resume of your achievements.

Identify the activity in which they are to take part. This eliminates the chance that some of them may not be attending the tour they think they are. It also tells the persons who have simply "joined up" what the tour is to be. If the tour is a part of an agency program, be sure to let the group know its name.

State the distance to be covered on the walk and the approximate time required. Some may not be able to make the tour due to physical limitations or lack of time. They should know what to expect before they begin the walk. Be sure that you adhere to the limitations you have indicated for distance and time. Getting back five minutes late is not too serious; arriving a half hour late is inexcusable.

Let them know where the walk is to end. This is especially important if it ends at a different place than where it began. It is most disconcerting to the visitor to find that the tour does not bring him back to his starting point, for he faces a walk back to his car or finding other transportation. He may have someone waiting for him to return. He may be operating on a time schedule with a bus or plane to catch, or he and his family may have planned to depart at a given time.

Inform the group of any special conditions to be met, such as rough terrain, or fees that may be charged while enroute. One such tour was found to require boat transportation as part of the walk. The fee for the boat was pretty costly, and several of the group went no farther than the boat dock. Understandably those people were much irritated by the turn of events.

Tell of any special gear that may be needed, such as warm clothing if entering a cave, etc. This is especially important when children are along, as worried parents do not contribute much to the group.

Briefly list some of the highlights to be expected, and the objectives of the walk. Your tour may be an ecological one dealing primarily with nature, or one centered around history, etc.

Invite members of the group to ask questions as the walk proceeds. Otherwise there may be some reluctance on their part to speak to you about things seen or mentioned.

Let them know how the walk is to be led. Do this tactfully, as you are setting up guide lines for them to follow, and you don't want to antagonize anyone. However, there have to be some observances of safety precautions, keeping the group together, the pace that will be set, etc.

3. The guided walk.

Begin the walk leisurely, moving only a short distance from the starting point before making your first stop. This stop should be within sight of where the tour began, which allows late comers to arrive and join. If the tour group is not in sight when late comers arrive, the chances are they will not attempt to overtake you. However, do not drag out the length of this stop.

Walk only as fast as the slowest in the group. Most visitors are not in the "pink" of condition. There may be older persons in the party who cannot move along at more than a leisurely pace. You will have to adjust your timing on the tour to the pace that can be set.

In leading the walk, keep in the lead at all times. Do not let individuals go ahead. Often children will want to run ahead of the party, but this should not be allowed to happen. A tactful approach will usually keep the youngsters in line without antagonizing parents. It should be kept in mind that if you do let them run ahead and an injury should occur, you may well be blamed for the incident.

In using a steep trail, take advantage of switchbacks. One big problem in handling a large tour group is getting them to a position where all can hear. This is difficult on a narrow trail, but if such a trail has switchbacks, it is good technique to stop the group after part of the party has made the turn, thus allowing everyone to hear what is said. If there is no switchback, you simply stop the group and walk back to the middle of the line, get off the trail (uphill if possible), and speak from this vantage point.

Be sure to collect your group before starting to talk. Too often tour leaders begin speaking before the end of the line has arrived. Naturally those persons miss the opening words about the point of interest at the stop. Failure to consider these persons is apt to cause them to leave the tour.

In talking to the group. speak clearly, don't talk too fast, and don't shout. Many people have difficulty in hearing, so it is important that you enunciate clearly. If you must shout to make yourself heard, you have stopped your party at the wrong place! Stopping close to a waterfall, beside a rushing stream, in a windy area, or near traffic sounds is not a good way to make yourself heard and understood.

Hopefully, stops along the tour route will generate discussions, but these should be kept simple. Don't let them lapse into academic treatments, and be sure to keep them on a level that all can understand. Don't lecture. Involve the group at least part of the time. Draw on listener experience when appropriate, but be prepared to shorten the time, if necessary.

Do not keep your group too long in one place, as many will become restless, and you will have lost some of the group interest you have been developing.

Keep your group together between stops. Don't let them scatter along the tour route. By all means, don't run away from them. Be safe at all times.

Handle humor with care. Planned humor is often easily recognized by the visitor, and sometimes such attempts border on the ridiculous. I recall one tour leader who asked his party, "Have you folks ever seen a tree toad?" No one had, so he walked over to a tree, placed his foot against the trunk, and observed: "Now you are seeing a tree toed!" Needless to say, he began to lose individuals from his party before the walk got very far. Don't be a wisecracker! If a comedian were needed on the tour, the employing agency or firm would undoubtedly have hired one! This does not mean you cannot have fun on the tour, but keep it spontaneous and of a type appreciated by all members.

As tour leader, don't choose certain people to cater to while on the trip. If you wear a uniform and are a man, you can be sure that elderly ladies and young girls are definitely "uniform" conscious. If you are a woman in uniform, you are likely to receive more than passing notice from men in the group.

If on a walk where plants may be part of your story, don't pick specimens to show to the group, as you are setting an example. If you pick plants, you may be sure your act is not overlooked by many on the tour.

Don't be a know-it-all. People resent a person whose attitude shows that he considers himself to be an expert.

Don't be afraid to say "I don't know." Too often a tour leader feels he will "lose face" if he doesn't know the answer to a question and will come up with some sort of a reply. Don't trap yourself! It is most deflating to one's ego to be caught with the wrong answer. No subject is ever so completely mastered that all the answers are known, and the average tour group can ask a vast assortment of questions on many subjects.

Never forget that you are on the tour to help the visitors, not to entertain them. You want them to enjoy themselves, of course, but your task is that of a helpful interpreter, not an amateur entertainer.

4. Termination of the walk.

As you approach the end of the tour, gather the group at a likely place and quickly review something of the scope and interests of the walk. This allows you to reemphasize important points you want them to be sure and remember. It also enables you to tie the entire tour together into a total picture.

If there are announcements to be made, this is the time to do it. Don't make them too lengthy. At this point, most members of the group are aware that the tour is ending and are ready to depart.

Dismiss the group; don't just let them drift away. Unless you do so, some will be reluctant to leave, fearing they will be discourteous. Invite any who wish to stay around with any questions they may have.

OTHER GUIDED TOURS

Two other guided tours, the auto caravan and the ski tour, should be mentioned. The former was once quite popular, but now is seldom used. Ski tours hold considerable promise for the future.

The auto caravan tour calls for special techniques in leading a line of cars. Many of those used on guided walks also apply to caravans. However, there are additional points that should be observed by the tour leader.

Be sure each driver is told how the caravan is to be handled and where it is going. A small tour map is most helpful to give to each driver.

If possible, form a line of cars as each one joins up for the tour. Don't let them simply park anywhere and then try to drop into line when the tour leaves.

Emphasize to each driver that passing is not permissible, although a car can leave the caravan at any time.

Stress safety to each driver. Specify the approximate distance you want between cars, and be sure the driver understands.

In pulling away from the meeting place, and also from all scheduled stops, signal that you are leaving and move out slowly. This allows all drivers to get motors started and form a line. Speed can then be slowly increased as the line starts moving. Thirty-five miles per hour is considered a safe cruising speed along most routes. Use your side-mounted rear view mirror to see that your group is moving properly. Be wary of side roads; someone in your caravan may decide to leave and he could "steal" the line of traffic behind him if you have it stretched out too much.

As you approach a scheduled stop, slow down gradually to allow possible stragglers to catch up. This also tells everyone that a stop is near.

Park your lead car so the middle section of your caravan is approximately even with the point of interest you will discuss. This allows everyone to get out of his car and walk only a short distance to reach the interest point. It eliminates much needless loss of time in getting the group out of cars and back in again.

At your final stop, let everyone know that you will be available for information as to return routes or other things the drivers may need to know.

With the growth of skiing in this country, guided ski tours offer fine interpretive possibilities in many areas. In addition to guiding techniques used on walking tours, the following points should be given consideration. Others will undoubtedly come to your mind depending upon the area chosen for the tour.

Choose a route that is not too difficult or strenuous. Some members of your group may not be too expert on skis or in the best physical condition. Don't make this a cross-country or mountain climbing expedition!

Your theme can be diversified, but the story of snow is an obvious one.

You are not restricted to formal constructed trails, so your route can visit points that are of unusual beauty in winter.

Watch for stragglers. Getting someone lost in a wilderness situation can be most unfortunate.

Carry a first aid kit. A sprained ankle is always a possibility and blisters are common.

Interpretation through Self-Guidance

CHAPTER 6
Self Guidance Methods and Devices

We often hear the statement "there is no substitute for the personal touch in interpretation." Perhaps this should be modified to say "no substitute for the personal touch in interpretation is of *equal value* insofar as the visitor is concerned." Certainly there are various self-guidance devices that are highly effective in telling the interpretive story. However, providing a supplementary interpretive service of this type should not be regarded as a complete replacement for the experience which the visitor receives through the warmth of personal service. A self-guiding trail or device, regardless of how well developed, is at best only a supplement to the human approach.

The self-guiding trail or tour might be defined as a type of visitor facility, consisting of an established physical route providing interpretation of area features, objects, structures or concepts by means of well designed devices located in sequence at selected sites. It is operated wholly, or in part, without personal services of interpretive personnel.

All unmanned interpretive devices are essentially self-guiding. These include exhibits of all types, regardless of location. They may be along roads, trails, at historic buildings, various types of structures, or even in museums.

A self-guiding facility should be developed to fill a specific interpretive need, and not simply because it is a popular device. Visitor use patterns and relationship of local features to the interpretive story to be told should dictate whether a self-guiding facility is logical and necessary to adequately interpret the area. Self-guidance should be related to and assist other interpretive facilities and services in telling the overall story. The facility should not be considered as a static installation, but should be designed for flexibility to allow for changing conditions, or inclusion of new knowledge.

To be really effective, the facility should provide the visitor with as many interpretive elements as possible. Such elements might include:

The story of human history and natural history seen along the route, told in a thematic way where possible.

Development of appreciation and understanding of the scenic, scientific and historic values of the area.

Recognition of inspirational values of the route of whatever nature.

Encouragement of an independent personal experience on the part of the visitor in some subject matter field.

Developing awareness of the visitor's own relationship to, and responsibility for, protection of the area, its features and environment.

Significance and meaning of the area, building, structure or site.

Creation of a truly enjoyable experience.

There are advantages and disadvantages to any type of interpretive activity, and certainly such are to be found in self-guiding facilities. Advantages would include:

"On-the-spot" interpretation. It is difficult for the visitor to carry in his mind interpretive material from an exhibit in a museum to the field site itself. On-site interpretation can show the object in its proper relationships, lending reality and vividness to the visitor's experience.

The visitor is given the opportunity for personal participation.

The visitor need not wait. He may go at any time with his activities controlled only by possible opening and closing hours of the area or structure.

He sets his own pace. This is important, as each person has his own interests, and will spend more time at some stops along the route than at others.

The visitor has some degree of privacy. He is not part of a large group, such as on a conducted tour.

The tour may be of a nature that encourages the timid and uninformed visitor to venture into unknown features of terrain with a feeling of security.

Less manpower is required in the interpretive operation.

The interpretive story can often be carried away by the visitor in the form of a small publication or leaflet.

Disadvantages to self-guiding devices include:

Lack of personal contact with a trained interpreter.

The facility cannot answer specific questions occurring to the visitor.

Advantage cannot be taken of the unexpected, such as a bear crossing the trail, a beautiful flower, etc.

They do not enable the visitor to follow up on specific interests.

The facility is often subject to vandalism.

It requires good maintenance to keep it in attractive and efficient operating condition.

Wayside exhibit, Grand Canyon National Park.

CLASSIFICATION OF SELF-GUIDING TRAILS OR TOURS

Just as guided tours are often classified by type, there are also several ways to classify self-guiding facilities. Such classifications are usually determined by the nature or character of the subject matter to be interpreted.

1. The specialized theme.

The primary characteristic is a single subject chosen for development to the exclusion of all others. It may be centered on history, archeology, natural history, ethnology, or man's activities. It may be restricted to one particular aspect of a subject, such as an historic event or date, ecology of a beaver pond, work of glaciers, or operation of a power dam. It may also be restricted to a specific process of man or nature, such as mining, weaving, tree growth, flour grinding, etc.

2. The "Great Truths" theme.

This concerns itself with a broad concept rather than a specific science, event or object. It may deal with life, philosophy, or the entities of history and science. Such subjects as the wholeness of nature, environment awareness, cultural development, the mind of man, etc., are representative of this type theme.

3. The opportunistic or theme-less.

The objective of this type of self-guiding facility may be to induce the visitor to become involved in the tour, to "read" the trailside, to become aware of objects seen along the route. It takes advantage of the many features encountered that the visitor might overlook, or the significance of which he may fail to understand. It presents a challenge to the visitor to probe even beyond what the tour has to offer.

4. The orientation theme.

This type of facility becomes interpretive in a minor way. For the most part, such a tour is designed to acquaint the visitor with geographic features and places. It gives him information about the places named, etc., rather than attempting to interpret them. There is no well devised story involved, nor does it apply any of the principles and laws of nature or social science. It is often used, however, to show relationships between places, such as portions of a battlefield and their relations to the terrain, relationship of high and low elevations, etc. It is primarily to inform the visitor.

Classification can also be made according to physical characteristics of each facility and the treatment given each. The physical characteristics indicate what kind of route or conveyance the facility utilizes; the treatment indicates by what method, or methods, the interpretive messages are to be made available to the visitor. Under physical characteristics would be such facilities as: foot trail, auto tour, boat tour, horse tour, underwater tour, house or structure tour, or combinations. Methods of treatment would include: numbered stake and booklet, text in place (includes signs and markers, labels, paintings, drawings and related subjects), the use of audio, and such devices as diagrams, models, objects, sighting tubes, and combination of various methods.

PLANNING THE SELF-GUIDING FACILITY

Planning a self-guiding facility is no simple matter, but neither does it require excessive time or experience. In the listings which follow are items that should always be considered in developing a well thought out program:

The facility should closely relate to existing operations, interpretive or otherwise. It should be an important and integral part of the overall scheme of interpretation for the area, and should be coordinated with all other phases of area operation.

Often its location is governed by the existence of a center of visitor concentration. A heavily visited feature, such as the General Sherman Tree in Sequoia National Park, immediately suggests additional visitor services through use of a well designed self-guiding trail featuring the sequoia story. Such facility is particularly valuable if other interpretive services in the general area are limited.

Self-guidance should normally not be established along a route served by a guided tour. To do so is duplication of effort, and each robs the other to some degree. This is especially noticeable where interpretive signs, markers, or exhibits are in place at points of interest along the route. Not only are such interpretive devices distractions on a guided tour, they also cause group confusion as visitors tend to divide attention between the tour leader and the self-guiding facility. If it is found desirable to establish both types of tours along the same route, unobtrusive numbered stakes and guide markers are certainly less objectionable than other devices.

The subject, or subjects, must be of intrinsic interest to the visitor, or capable of being made interesting by skillful interpretation. Even unrelated stations of a "themeless" trail or tour can be made meaningful when there is continuity or connection between points. What may appear to be unimpressive material can be developed into an outstanding facility through perception, imagination and "feel" for its interpretive story.

Subjects that are ephemeral in character, such as blooming flowers, must be handled in a way to make their identification and interpretation flexible. There is nothing so frustrating to the visitor as to be given good identification, only to find that the flower has long since bloomed and gone.

Existence and location of key features, objects or structures to be interpreted are often basic and may determine the route to be followed and the spacing of points of interest.

Where possible, planning the location of self-guiding facilities should be worked out when trail, road routes or other physical developments are programmed.

Safety of the route chosen is very important. Dangerous situations should be avoided by careful study of the area. The route should not be physically strenuous, or have rough sections. This forestalls possible tort claims.

The self-guiding facility should be easily accessible and readily seen by the visitor if it is to render maximum service.

Adequate parking space must be available at, or near, the start of the tour. This is especially important if the self-guiding facility is some distance from developed areas.

Landscape and aesthetic values should be considered in the route selection. Interpretive devices along the way should not intrude conspicuously upon the scene, features or any structures.

Go over the proposed route several times to grasp its full potential before final selection.

While self-guiding trails or tours receive much heavier use when located near normal routes of visitor travel, this does not mean that all such facilities must be so located. Occasionally a trail to an outstanding scenic, historic or scientific feature can easily be justified.

LAYING OUT THE TRAIL OR TOUR

Among the most important points to keep in mind when laying out the self-guiding trail or tour are the following:

A well chosen name is an asset. It can be used to give a clue to the visitor as to what is featured along the route. The title should be pleasing to read, inviting, and easily remembered. Such titles as "Trail of the Shadows," "Cactus Forest Drive," and "The Hallowed Ground" are familiar examples. The title should be on an attractive and conspicuous sign at the point where the tour begins, and in harmony with its surroundings. Such a name says to the visitor, "Here is something of unusual interest."

A self-guiding trail should not be straight. Use of curves along the route lends interest and increases a feeling of privacy. Even a heavily used facility can seem rather remote if enough screening is available.

Each self-guiding facility should have a well defined beginning and end. Where possible both should occur at, or near to, the same point. This is important if the facility is a trail; it may not be possible, however, with a facility laid out as a road tour.

Be sure the route is physically easy to follow. The visitor should never have any doubt as to where the trail or tour makes the next turn.

The first interpretive marker, numbered stake or other device used to indicate the location of the point of interest should be within sight of the starting point. This also serves as an invitation to undecided persons. This provision does not hold true if the facility is an auto tour.

Spacing of signs and markers along the route should be close enough to sustain interest, but not so close that visitors are likely to intrude on each other. Where possible, the spacing between markers should be relatively even, with no lengthy gaps. They should always be placed along the edge of the route. If located some distance from it, they may be overlooked.

The sign or marker should be close enough to an object being interpreted that there is no chance for mistaken identification, yet not so close as to detract from its appearance or use as a photographic subject.

In placing signs and markers along an auto tour route, consideration should be given to the presence or absence of a formal parking place, "pull outs," the nature of road curves, sight distance and other safety factors.

There are different opinions as to how many numbered or named stations should be included in a self-guiding facility. However, a well balanced trail will have 20–30 points of interest selected for interpretation; the road tour a few less.

The most desirable length of the trail or tour varies greatly, depending upon the extent of the area to be interpreted, number of features to be visited, energy that must be expended by the visitor, length of time the visitor normally spends in the area, weather conditions to be expected, and visitor use patterns. Most successful walking tours seldom exceed one mile in length, with two miles a maximum.

Where terrain is a problem, a self-guiding trail should have any necessary uphill travel near the beginning of the tour, if at all possible, with downhill walking on the return. Facing an uphill climb toward the end of a walk is somewhat dismaying to the poorly conditioned visitor.

Call attention to outstanding photographic opportunities along the route, for many visitors carry cameras.

Place benches at appropriate spots, where possible. View points, shady spots and natural rest sites make ideal locations, and the visitor will appreciate your thoughtfulness.

If the self-guiding facility uses leaflets or booklets, a distribution box is necessary at or near the starting point; or they may be given out at a visitor center. If the tour publication is offered for sale, a vandal-proof coin box or vending machine is required. Care should be taken to see that contents of the dispensing box or device are protected from damage by rain or snow.

TYPES OF SELF-GUIDING DEVICES

Those with the greatest effectiveness are grouped somewhat as follows:

1. Physical aids in place.
    a. The stake and interpretive label method.
    b. The underwater trail.
    c. The interpretive sign.
    d. The wayside exhibit.
    e. The outdoor display method.

2. Physical aids, with self-guiding literature.
    a. The stake and leaflet method.
    b. Self-guiding boat tours.
    c. Marine garden tours.
    d. Back country tours.

Painted wood, self-guiding signs. Left-Tongass National Forest. Right-Yosemite National Park.

3. Physical aids with recorded messages.

    a. Trail and road tours.

    b. Garden and building tours.

    c. Radio transmittals and on-site repeaters.

4. Physical aids, combinations of items 1, 2 and 3.

5. Special uses of physical aids.

    a. Symbols.

    b. Statement of trail or tour objective.

    c. Trail map.

    d. Aids to visitor traffic.

    e. Restoration drawings, diagrams.

While there are numerous ways to accomplish self-guidance, the most successful are found in a somewhat select group using simple, uncomplicated methods. Their success is due to the ease with which visitors can use them, and the effectiveness with which their interpretive messages can be absorbed. Almost as an after thought, they are usually inexpensive to develop and put into operation. Only the special devices tend to incur much additional expense.

Whether used as a self-guided boat or auto tour, a trailside experience, or a leisurely stroll through history, most self-guiding facilities have certain basic characteristics common to all. Thus, they differ in method, but not in objectives. To understand more fully the characteristics, advantages and disadvantages of the best known types, let us examine each in turn.

PHYSICAL AIDS IN PLACE

1. The stake and interpretive label method.

This type of self-guidance is commonly encountered, whether in the many natural parks across our country, in the forests, or in the more formalized city parks. Basically it consists of a relatively short interpretive message mounted on a stake, and placed by, or near to, some object, feature or structure that is deemed to have a story worthy of telling. It may also be used strictly for orientation and limited to name, location, dates, etc.

The stake (post or other device) is usually of wood, metal or concrete, tall enough that the visitor doesn't have to stoop to read the message it carries, yet short enough not to constitute an intrusion.

The interpretive message may be routed, typed, printed, lettered, painted, reproduced photographically, or cast in metal or concrete. The label or marker may be made of metal, plastic, wood, concrete, stone, treated paper, or any number of combinations.

The message text may carry several details of a story, or there may be no text at all, simply diagrams to show relationships, or photographs to identify a plant, object, structure or landscape scene. Text should have letters large enough for easy reading, as many visitors find it difficult to read with bifocal or trifocal glasses. Color and background of lettering is an important consideration. Writing text for this type of sign is an art in itself, and few do it really well. There is need for short sentences, non-scientific terminology, and accepted nomenclature of such things as flowers, etc. The label should also be understandable, interesting and completely accurate, both in fact and spelling.

Advantages are, in part:

It is very effective when the trail or tour is of considerable length.

Visitors often do not wish to carry descriptive literature along; thus, on-site labels are well received.

It is not difficult to modify a label to reflect seasonal changes or include new knowledge.

It is normally not very expensive to replace vandalized labels.

Among disadvantages are:

A good supply of spare stakes and accompanying label texts must be kept on hand. There is normally attrition through vandalism or the work of pranksters. A large number of such labels have a way of finding new usage as adornments in student rooms on various school campuses.

Loss of a single label may impair the continuity of the interpretive story being told.

Constant maintenance is essential, not only to correct man-caused damage, but to counteract results of weathering.

A label can be an intrusion on a wilderness situation, and care must be exercised in its design.

The label text is physically located at a definite site, and the interested visitor must either remember its message or copy it for future reference. He cannot take it with him, although many instances are reported where he tried!

2. The underwater trail.

With growth of interest in the marine world, this type of facility is experiencing growing popularity. It has the same basic objectives as the stake and interpretive label method, but is used by the swimmer or wader in water situations where there is a story to be told. It is usually accomplished by producing interpretive labels that can be anchored beneath the water at selected sites. (See chapter on underwater interpretation).

The signs may be routed, cast or painted. Text letters must be large enough for easy reading by the visitor using a face mask, or by looking down through the water from the surface.

3. The interpretive sign.

Basically this device is merely an enlargement of the interpretive label. It is larger in size, longer in text, and designed to tell a more complete story in itself. It is usually placed on much more substantial mountings, and stands higher above the ground than the interpretive label.

It must be attractive to do an effective job. A poorly designed sign, both as to color and shape, is not acceptable. It must have a finished look and "eye" appeal. It must be made of materials in harmony with its surroundings, yet clearly visible. Various types of materials are available, so be sure to select the best for your purpose. (See section on Producing Self-guiding Signs, Markers and Literature).

What are the ingredients for the text of a good interpretive sign? Here are some basics:

It should have an attention-getting lead-in statement, and an equally interesting closing thought.

It must be simple. It should never contain statements that require much, if any explanation.

It must be only long enough to present the message.

It must be "readable."

It must be easily understood. If the reader has to figure out what you are saying, it has failed.

It must not contain words whose meanings are not usually known.

It should not be slangy.

It must be friendly in tone and content.

The content of the message should be imaginative in treatment.

The message should be an entity unto itself, yet tie in with the overall area interpretive story.

It should not be controversial in nature.

It should have a "teaser" thought, if possible, to stimulate further study.

It should leave the reader with an urge to check further.

Any humor, if used at all, should be handled with extreme care.

4. The wayside exhibit.

This type of device is also commonly referred to as a trailside exhibit or an on-site exhibit. It is used where more detailed treatment is needed. It may cover the total story of the site, thus serving as an entity in itself. It may contain actual display objects, sketches and charts, which may or may not be "native" to the site. It may be relatively large, or of more simple design. Basically it is a structure normally used to display exhibits behind glass. It may have one or several glass panels, and is roofed for protection against inclement weather and sun.

Some advantages of the wayside exhibit are:

It attracts visitors and will almost certainly entice them to see what is being presented.

It allows for detailed presentation of a subject, at a location where it can be most effective.

It can handle rather large numbers of visitors in a limited time.

It is especially effective along trails of a mile or more in length, and at road pull-outs.

It is much appreciated by visitors who do not carry descriptive literature with them.

Disadvantages include:

The device is more costly to construct than most out-of-door interpretive facilities.

Preparation and installation of the exhibit is more expensive than for some other methods.

The device must be inspected at fairly frequent intervals to keep it in good condition. Inspection is especially critical after the winter season is over.

Maintenance costs are relatively higher than for most other out-of-door devices.

It is somewhat difficult, and more expensive, to alter or improve the exhibits once they are installed.

Vandalism is a problem unless special precautions are taken. Unlike a sign or marker that can be easily removed and carried away, the exhibit is subject to damage or total destruction.

Loss of one such exhibit may seriously impair or destroy interpretive value of the site.

If located along a trail used for guided tours, it becomes a distraction. Members of such a group tend to direct their attention to the exhibit, and thus break continuity of the tour leader's presentation.

5. The outdoor display.

Occasionally there arises need to develop a display in an out-of-doors situation using plants, rocks and historic or pre-historic objects or structures assembled in such manner as to tell a comprehensive story. This allows many items to be brought together that would otherwise be difficult to utilize because of original location in widely separated spots. By putting all these together, it is possible to present a compre-hensive concept, process or even a culture. Through the use of interpretive labels in a garden or outdoor exhibit area, the story can be told in a clear and meaningful way. This type of self-guidance can be used wherever it is found desirable and logical.

Its primary weakness lies in the fact that it is definitely an unnatural situation, and might possibly be confused for the original condition. It also tends to be limited in subject mat-ter, with emphasis usually falling on botanical, geological, historical or archeological items..

PHYSICAL AIDS, WITH SELF-GUIDING LITERATURE

1. The stake and leaflet method.

This is the method most commonly used over much of the country. Thus far it has been considered one of the most useful devices in terms of cost, effectiveness and simplicity. It is popular with both the one who designs it and the visitor who uses it.

Basically it involves selection of interpretive sites along an established route, which are then marked with numbered stakes, posts or other markers. A leaflet, or small booklet, is then produced to tell the interpretive story of each site.

Methods of marking vary considerably, depending on the type of route to be covered and locations of the numbered stakes or markers. Some areas prefer rustic posts with the numbers routed, printed or burned into the horizontal, verti-cal or angled surfaces. Some use posts or stakes made of wood, metal, or even concrete, with cast, metal screw-on, or slip-in numbers. Stone markers have also been used with engraved or painted numbers. Some markers simply bear the name of the site or object being interpreted, and the accompanying leaflet or booklet utilizes the location name to identify interpretive text.

A wide variety of literature may be found in various parks, forests, etc., but basically all operate on the same principle. Booklets and leaflets are designed to tell the interpretive story in sufficient detail to be easily understood, and, at the same time, allow the visitor to take the material away with him. A box for dispensing the leaflet or booklet is usually required, and is located near the start of the tour. Some publications are distributed at a visitor center or museum rather than at the self-guiding device.

This method, although simple to produce and operate, has numerous advantages and disadvantages. Among advantages are:

Inexpensive materials can be used for both the location marker and the publication.

Such a system is easy to design and install.

It is possible for the writer to prepare the text for "out loud" reading designed for family groups who use the facility.

It is easy to rearrange if found desirable.

It is simple to replace materials lost or destroyed.

Vandalism is normally not a great problem. Removal, defacement or destruction of a site marker does not have much appeal to the occasional vandal.

Intrusion upon the natural or historic scene is minimal. While the site markers must be seen to be effective, appearance is easy to control.

Because the markers are unobtrusive, they do not conflict too much with guided walks or tours that may use the same route.

A trail with numbered stakes and an interpretive publication guide gives the timid visitor a sense of security and safety. This is especially valuable if the trail passes through heavy forest or wild country.

A marked route tends to keep visitors on the established trail, minimizing the tendency to wander or short cut.

Even if the marker is lost or stolen, the leaflet or booklet carried by the visitor gives him an unbroken story.

The publication can be taken by the visitor for future reference or as a souvenir of his visit.

Disadvantages are not especially numerous, but they include:

As in all self-guidance, some vandalism is to be expected, even though not extensive.

There is need for regular maintenance to assure attractive appearing markers.

Where the small booklets are for sale, there is some loss from visitors who simply take them without payment.

Free booklets and leaflets tend to encourage littering, especially of the latter. The psychology seems to be if the literature does not cost anything, it isn't worth keeping!

2. The self-guiding boat tour.

This is a field in which little has been done over much of the country, but there is considerable potential. With a well designed boating guide the boat traveler can readily identify prominent topographic features along the seashore, lake or river. The interpretive stories can thus be keyed to these features. It is also possible to use a number system along the shoreline at key points. These can be made visible from the boat by contrasting color background or a unique shape to the marker. They should not be glaringly evident, but visible to the traveler wishing to locate them.

3. The marine garden tour.

This type of tour must be carefully done to be effective in a seacoast situation. Posts must be placed to withstand tides and still be visible when the tide is out and the marine gardens are exposed. The problem of salt-water deterioration of markers is always present.

4. Back country tours.

With an ever increasing number of hikers utilizing back country regions, there is need to develop self-guiding devices which will assist these people. A small, pocket-size booklet can be produced whose interpretive messages are keyed to readily recognized topographic or other features shown on trail map sections. Such a booklet will necessarily have to be distributed at some central point of visitor contact, such as a visitor center or museum.

PHYSICAL AIDS WITH RECORDED MESSAGES

The tape recorded interpretive message has brought a new dimension into self-guidance. It may be used in a number of ways, the most common being the following:

1. Trail and road tours.

A portable play-back device, equipped with cassette type tape, is used in lieu of a booklet or leaflet. The interpretive message is recorded. The location of each interpretive site may be indicated by a numbered marker or descriptive narration on the tape. The visitor has only to activate the play-

Self-guiding auto tour tape recorded with a portable repeater, Lake Mead National Recreation Area.

back device to obtain the various interpretive messages along the route.

2. Garden and building tours.

Produced in the same manner as above and used in much the same way. However, the interpretive narrative tends to be more general in nature.

3. Radio transmittals and on-site repeaters.

Tape recorded interpretive messages are transmitted by short range radio to cars traveling along the road. The car radio serves as the receiver.

A tape repeater with recorded message is located within a permanent structure and activated by push button. The device is normally placed only at special sites and serves both the visitor using self-guidance and one who is not.

Among the advantages of this method are:

It requires no reading of literature or signs, merely the ability to listen and follow directions.

Considerably more information can be given to the visitor than could be included in a small booklet or leaflet.

The narrator's voice can be used to give emphasis to portions of the interpretive message deemed of special importance.

Tape recordings can be easily changed to include new knowledge or improve the old narrative.

Disadvantages are not many, but are quite important. They include:

The equipment needed to bring the taped message to the visitor tends to be rather expensive.

Maintenance of equipment is essential at all times.

The equipment used with on-site repeaters is subject to weather damage and possible vandalism.

PHYSICAL AIDS, COMBINATIONS

Combining the above methods, along with utilizing such things as exhibits, objects, or structures, is also very effective. Areas featuring history or archeology have found this especially helpful. Primarily it may involve any of the above methods used in combination with any significant object or structure along the route. Wayside exhibits, interpretive markers and on-site taped messages may also become a part of the planned route, and an integral part of the overall interpretive story.

Advantages of such a method would include the following:

It allows use of detailed exhibits at special points of interest occurring along the route.

Continuous use of a leaflet or booklet is not required. This allows for a "change of pace" which the visitor often appreciates.

It still contains the basic simplicity of the other self-guidance methods.

Disadvantages are few, but very important:

There is some loss of flexibility where fixed exhibits are used. These cannot be easily altered to meet changing conditions.

The visitor is unable to take away with him the story told in the fixed exhibit, unless it is repeated in the leaflet or booklet describing the tour.

If formalized exhibits are used, they tend to eliminate visitor feeling of being in an undisturbed environment.

SPECIAL USES OF PHYSICAL AIDS

Various devices and techniques should also be considered as the route is developed. Most of these are simple, yet add much to success of the facility. Some of the most important are:

1. Symbols.

These devices are designed to arouse the visitor's interest in a trail or tour. It acquaints him with existence of the facility when he might otherwise miss it. The symbol chosen should, if possible, be representative of the area or park in which it is found. For example, in Yosemite National Park a simple, routed profile of Half Dome is placed on each tour marker along the highways. The wooden marker also carries the number of the interest point. Along the Blue Ridge Parkway, the symbol is a sketch of a squirrel rifle and powder horn. In Sequoia National Park it is twin sequoia cones. Such a symbol tells the visitor that here is something of unusual interest, and he may look more closely for other such indicators. Sometimes the symbol is used along the highways to announce the approach of a turn-out containing a point of interest, or to alert the driver that he is approaching a numbered marker or named feature.

2. Statement of the trail or tour objective.

Lacking a personal means of introducing the visitor to the self-guiding trail or tour, it is often valuable to present a brief statement through use of an attractive routed sign or similar device at the point where the tour begins. The statement may be used in conjunction with the sign bearing the name of the tour, if found desirable. It can also be used as an opening paragraph for the self-guiding booklet or leaflet. Its function is simple: to arouse the visitor's interest to the point where he wants to take the tour. The statement should be short and carefully worded. It should appeal to the imagination, yet not belittle one's intelligence. For example, the name of a self-guiding trail might be "The Trail of Pinnacles" and the ac-

**Self-guiding trail numbering
method, Walnut Canyon
National Monument.**

companying statement might read "A Walk Through 15 Million Years of Time." Or, in a more lengthy fashion it might read: "The Gentian Trail. It will lead you through quiet and pleasant surroundings, rich in plant life and geological interest. Wayside labels will help make your walk more enjoyable."

3. The trail map.

Sometimes it is most helpful to place a routed or painted trail or tour map at the start of the route. This enables the visitor to visualize the entire route, the distance to be covered, and some of the key points to be visited. A statement as to normal walking or driving time is also helpful. This information often makes the difference as to whether or not the visitor will take the tour.

4. Aids to visitor traffic.

Often it is very important that traffic move on a predetermined course. This is especially true for indoor situations, and may be accomplished through use of directional arrows, interpretive messages or labels at doorways, or by using unobtrusive barriers to steer the visitor along the desired route. The small directional arrow is also very effective on out-of-door tours.

5. Restoration drawings, diagrams and paintings.

This type of interpretive aid is most helpful to show how a building or feature may have looked originally, and is very useful in historical and archeological areas. The drawing or painting can be used as a small trailside exhibit, or put in the interpretive leaflet or booklet. Diagrams are valuable in showing geological relationships of various formations, and in naming geographic features seen from the site being interpreted.

PRODUCING SELF-GUIDING SIGNS, MARKERS AND LITERATURE

The best planned trail or tour may be reduced in its effectiveness by poorly produced physical aids. Visitors are swayed by appearance of a facility. One that is neat and attractive not only invites visitor use, but encourages good care and treatment. A facility that looks run down and neglected may receive little consideration by the user. In production of these physical aids, the local staff in an area can usually be depended upon to do much of its own design, and sometimes even construction. Some areas are fortunate enough to have skilled technicians who can do any type of sign work, but often this must be done by outside firms.

In preparing signs and markers, a check should be made of possible sources for the latest materials on the market, as new products are constantly being developed. However, the following suggestions are made of materials that have proven most valuable:

1. Routed materials.

Without doubt the most popular and economical sign thus far produced is the one routed into wood or some other material. Several kinds of wood have proved satisfactory, but redwood and "cedar" are two of the best. Redwood is a favorite with many areas because it is easy to work, is attractive, economical, stands adverse weather, and tends to harmonize with its surroundings. The lettering is easy to read. It does not have sun glare. However, one should not overlook the field of laminated plastics. Such material is especially useful when small letters are used in a label or sign. The plastic tends to be weather and vandal resistant, and is not expensive. It is especially effective as inlays in wooden signs, and can be obtained in a wide variety of base colors and cores. It does tend to expand and contract from temperatures, and may crack at the corners if too tight in a metal frame. Sometimes sun glare must be considered. Some colors tend to fade when out-of-doors.

In those areas where vandalism is a problem, use of the routed aluminum sign is an important consideration. It is attractive, durable, tends to be vandal resistant—and is rather costly. In making this type of sign, it should be specified that the surface be sand etched before routing is done. This eliminates sun glare, and discourages scratching of the surface by vandals and thoughtless visitors.

Metalphoto interpretive sign,
Aztec National Monument.

2. Painted signs and markers.

These usually have to be made by a commercial sign painter. It is thus more expensive than routing, as special skills are necessary to produce attractive letters. Type of lettering and size used are very important. Larger letters are required if the label is to be read from a car; smaller letters are desirable if the message is to be read along a walking route. Letter style is important, also. Script and Old English harmonize with historical subjects, but would be out of place with natural history. Care must also be exercised in choosing background for the letters, as white will cause glare on out-door signs. Soft tones in tan or green are best for sunny situations. Maintenance and replacement of such signs is rather costly.

3. Cast metal signs.

Metal signs are not only vandal resistant, but stand adverse weather very well. The two most popular types are aluminum and bronze. Cast aluminum can be obtained in a variety of colors. Such a sign is relatively easy to maintain, and so hard as to make vandalism difficult. It is especially appropriate in historical and archeological areas. Entire scenes or drawings of structures can readily be produced by this method.

4. Printed signs on metal.

The product by the trade name of Metalphoto is best known at present and has many uses. Basically the process involves the placement on a metal plate of pictures and text through photographic techniques. It has several advantages:

It is attractive.

Almost any kind of photo, chart or drawing can be reproduced in detail.

It is weather resistant, little affected by climate, winds, flying dust, etc.

It is vandal resistant.

It is easy to produce and not expensive.

It works well in combination with other materials.

Naturally there are some disadvantages, but fortunately very few:

It is usually made commercially and not in an area darkroom.

It does have some sun glare in outdoor situations.

5. Multilithed signs and markers.

For the area short on funds, this type of sign can be produced at minimal expense. This method is especially useful to show diagrams, photographs, drawings, etc., usually accompanied by a short text. The finished sheet can be glued onto a board or other material and covered with clear varnish, liquid tile, or embedding plastics and resins. It may also be made into a clear plastic "sandwich." If it becomes soiled or damaged in some way, it is easy to replace. This method also helps "test run" a new self-guiding trail or tour before going into a more detailed and expensive treatment.

6. The interpretive leaflet or booklet.

Self-guiding literature becomes an important tool of interpretation when well written and attractively produced. It is an effective substitute for the interpreter himself, although not a complete one. It has several important advantages over interpretive signs and exhibits. It offers greater flexibility in subject matter. It makes possible a wide variety of illustrations, including photographs, sketches, diagrams, maps and drawings. It can utilize color in its printing to increase reader interest, at the same time making it more desirable as a take home item. Revision and updating are easy to accomplish with each reprinting. Its use along the tour route affords more versatility than a fixed sign. The reader can always refer back to features along the route. It presents an unbroken story, even if a station marker has been removed.

Writing the booklet or leaflet is somewhat different from other interpretive publications. Most of them spend considerable text, illustrations and time reconstructing a scene, or describing a feature or structure. However, the writer of the self-guiding booklet must keep in mind that the *real thing* is in view of the visitor as he reads, so there is less need for extensive descriptive text and illustrations. No picture is as good as the actual scene.

Writing a self-guiding booklet for an auto tour is not quite the same as for a self-guiding trail or walking tour. The people in the auto tour are likely to stay in their car and read, if at all possible to do so. Sometimes the car is not even stopped at a roadside marker, and the booklet is read as the visitors proceed on down the road. Because of these things, brevity and clarity are vital. This calls for easily read text, and the designation of marker numbers must be conspicuous for quick identification. Bold face type or underlining of captions becomes important. The type of paper used in the booklet is a consideration. Slick and coated paper are attractive, but cost is high and the glossy surface produces excessive glare if used in sunlight. Because most tours, whether by car, boat, or on foot are usually carried on out-of-doors—often in all sorts of weather—a medium weight, uncoated paper is preferable.

There are a number of simple precautions the writer should consider when preparing text. If he observes them, he is likely to come out with a rather well written manuscript. Basically he should remember the old saying: "Write unto others as you would have them write unto you!"

As suggestions:

Select words that are simple and easily understood; shrink them where possible.

Don't be slangy, as people often resent it. This doesn't mean you should not be human.

Don't be wordy, but get to the meat of the subject quickly. This is not the place to show the extent of your knowledge of the subject.

Avoid unfamiliar terms and technical language; such can be confusing.

Don't go into superlatives. You are not preparing a sales pitch for the reader.

Don't be stuffy. This is not the place to demonstrate your knowledge of the English language.

Use short sentences and short paragraphs. The most effective sentence length is around 17–19 words.

Be sure your thoughts are well tied together.

Make your writeup friendly in tone. This is your way of "speaking" to the reader.

Use active rather than passive verbs when possible.

Avoid such impersonal words and phrases as "it is believed" or "authorities have found."

Take care that the picture you are creating in the reader's mind cannot be taken the wrong way.

Use good punctuation, as it helps to make your meaning clear.

Have just one idea in each sentence, otherwise you can confuse the reader.

With a well thought-out route, attractive and appealing markers and signs, plus thoughtfully written booklets, self-guidance is one of the most effective and rewarding interpretive devices.

Other Interpretive Methods and Facilities

CHAPTER 7

Other Interpretive Methods

There are at least two types of interpretive activities that merit special consideration. One is the matter of using demonstrations to put across an idea; the other is designing and carrying out interpretation in underwater situations.

INTERPRETATION THROUGH DEMONSTRATIONS

Demonstrations as part of an interpretation are not used nearly enough. This is regrettable, as it is one of the most effective methods available to give the visitor a clear understanding of what is being interpreted. Various reasons why this is so shows up when a going program is reviewed. Usually the reason is simple; no one happened to think of any activity where a demonstration was the obvious answer. There is also the interpreter who is unsure of himself, or simply reluctant to "put on a show" before a group of people. Many an interpreter can give an acceptable performance, if all he has to do is give an oral presentation, but the thought of showing as well as telling is disturbing to him.

This does not mean, of course, that a demonstration is essential to a good interpretive program. Rather, a demonstration offers a good tool for the interpreter to use. It should be obvious that it does not fit every situation, and must be used selectively. It must be tastefully presented, as anything with a "side show" atmosphere will strike the visitor as being cheap. However, there is danger in it being too attractive for it must not detract from the main values of the park, area, or structure being interpreted. It must be pertinent to the main story, not simply an entertaining entity by itself. It should be kept relatively simple, if possible, although involved ones can be effective when well done.

As a device it has many values:

It offers the visitor an opportunity to see one or more phases of the story as well as hear about it.

It encourages questions.

It holds visitor attention. Seldom does one find the visitor indifferent to a good demonstration.

It can show the involved story when an oral description would be very inadequate.

It shows clearly how something is done.

It shows clearly how something works.

It offers the interpreter an opportunity to involve one or more visitors in the program by using him as part of the demonstration. Thus, the visitor becomes part of the tour and not simply a spectator. Some care must be exercised here, however, as the visitor must be a willing aid in the demonstration, and not a reluctant participant.

It offers the interpreter an opportunity to get children on the tour involved, thus furnishing them an experience they will long remember. Children are natural born play actors, and take to demonstrations in which they are a part. For example, at one of the military parks, the historian in charge of the tour wanted to ex-

Demonstration of a pioneer-type farm, Great Smokey Mountain National Park.

plain how a Civil War cannon was fired. He explained the operation by selecting youngsters from the tour group and designating them as the gun crew. He had each child play the part of some member of the crew and explained what each was to do. Then, he had his crew "load" the cannon, and when all was ready, the imaginary lanyard was pulled and the cannon "fired," with the youngsters even furnishing the noise! There is a precaution that must always be followed in a situation such as this; the entire operation must be safe for all concerned.

There are many places where a demonstration ordinarily can be used to advantage. Historical and archeological areas offer the finest opportunities. In Jamestown, Virginia, a fine demonstration shows the visitors how glass is blown. In many areas the events or life of an historical period are portrayed by persons in costume. This type of demonstration is often referred to as "living history." In an archeological area, visitors were shown the use of the atlatl, the throwing stick of early Indian hunters. In another area, use of the pecking stone by Indians was demonstrated. Sometimes visitors are shown how arrowheads were made, and in Yosemite an Indian woman showed how to make acorn bread. These are only a few imaginative uses of the demonstration where history,

Left-Demonstration of crafts. "Living History," City of Refuge National Monument, Hawaii. Right-Small animal life **can be used effectively in trailside demonstrations—a salamander, Kings Canyon National Park.**

archeology and Indian culture were important subjects to be interpreted.

Naturalists have an equally wide open field for use of demonstrations. Again, it is a matter of good imaginative subjects. Show how an ant lion works, put a horned lizard to "sleep," pour water on "resurrection moss," call birds to the group by making provocative sounds, strike rocks together to demonstrate the sulphur-like smell—these are a few of the many things that can be shown in the natural history world. The world of smell, feel and taste, seldom used in interpretation, offers a wide open field for good demonstrations.

Sometimes we find demonstrations that involve use of live specimens, and here we should inject a note of caution. Be very sure that what you are holding for the visitor to see is not dangerous. Snakes, for example, even harmless ones, usually affect many of your visitors adversely, and an enjoyable tour can be spoiled for them by any demonstration involving this type of animal life. The same can be said about spiders and several other small forms.

A good example of what not to do once happened in one of our National Parks. A group of visitors was hiking up a canyon with a naturalist leading the party. Right in the middle of the trail he discovered a rattlesnake. Now this man knew snakes and he felt this would be a good time to demonstrate a few things about poisonous snakes. Accordingly, he pinned the snake's head down and grasped it behind the head. Raising it up he showed the group. Some backed away in a big hurry, others came closer for a good look. Then something happened that wasn't in the script. The snake managed to get its head loose just enough to sink its fangs into the guide's hand. That, of course, brought horrified screams from some members of the party, and excited everyone. Help was some distance away. At this point the naturalist salvaged what appeared to be a disaster for him. He had everyone sit down. Then he calmly took out a pocket knife, made an incision in the bite, applied pressure to make the wound bleed, and used a handkerchief as a tourniquet. All the time he kept up a running description of why he was doing all these things, and how the poison was acting on his hand! His calmness settled everyone down. Then he selected one of the party to go for help, and sat down with the rest of the party to wait. Periodically he loosened the tourniquet and explained what was happening with the bite. The arrival of a doctor with anti-venin brought the entire incident to a happy conclusion. There was no doubt the entire demonstration had been effective, but most unnecessary and undesirable! It did, of course, underscore need to always select a safe demonstration.

Take a good look around where you are carrying on your interpretive program, and you will likely find some excellent opportunities to show as well as tell. Certainly the visitors will enjoy demonstrations if in good taste.

UNDERWATER INTERPRETATION

One of the most encouraging trends in interpretation to emerge in recent years has come with growing interest in the underwater world. This is not to say that it has been ignored, because various commercial and non-commercial endeavors have made the public increasingly aware of this great field of interest.

Underwater activities have reached a high level of public acceptance, especially in Florida and Texas.

There has also been a great increase in such activities as scuba diving, snorkeling and the always popular swimming. However, activities designed primarily to interpret the marine environment to the visitor are a more recent development. This is reflected by growing interest in underwater interpretation by both Federal and State agencies. Underwater national parks are now being established; State parks have also been established featuring a marine environment.

Underwater auditorium — the fixed structure, Weeki Waschi Springs.

For many years aquatic interpretation in the parks, both State and National, centered primarily upon such things as exhibits of native fishes and the like. Special animal forms were interpreted to the public, such as the blind fishes at Mammoth Cave National Park, the tiny pupfish at Death Valley National Monument and the California gray whale at Cabrillo National Monument. There were aquariums and fish ponds, even fish exhibits in lakes. Numerous interpretive publications, primarily on fishes, were also produced. In the meantime private enterprises, such as Silver Springs, Wicki Waschi and Homosassa Springs—all in Florida—were trying out underwater structures and techniques that could be made into highly effective interpretive devices.

Now there is developing broad recognition that there are as many unique and interesting underwater seascapes and animal forms as are found in dry land parks and forests. With this recognition comes the question of how to most effectively interpret such marine areas.

Certainly there is no one "best" way to do it. Just as on dry land, there are numerous methods and techniques from which to choose, and more are being developed as creative imagination examines possibilities. Effectiveness of methods and devices used today will be challenged, and perhaps rendered less important during the next few years. Certainly one of the greatest problems to overcome is that of actually showing the visitor what is beneath the surface of the water. With that in mind, let us review some methods and devices now in use:

1. The use of special boats.

Used in the past, and still popular in many areas, is the glass-bottom boat. This facility has several attractive features:

It is mobile and can easily be moved from one viewing point to another. This enables the viewing party to see a fairly wide area with minimal effort.

The people on board can hear what the interpreter is saying, so short talks at key points of underwater interest are easily accomplished. The visitor may also ask questions and hear answers with no difficulty.

The boat lends a sense of safety and security to the visitor who tends to be timid and a bit afraid of the unfamiliar environment.

Several people can be given interpretation simultaneously.

It can usually operate in relatively shallow water.

There are also limitations on the use of this device:

Its primary use is for "looking down."

The viewing area is rather limited, as most boats of this nature are restricted in size.

Such a boat is less effective in deeper water.

Its usefulness is pretty much restricted to reasonably quiet water. Waves, even small ones, diminish the boat's effectiveness.

Very little can be seen laterally from the boat.

Another type is the porthole boat. This allows the visitor to see from *beneath* the water surface. The visitor simply goes down into the hull of the boat, and through rows of glass-covered portholes views the underwater scene as the boat moves along. Such a boat is usually powered with an electric motor that can be turned 365 degrees for steering and maneuvering purposes. Some advantages are:

The visitor sits comfortably in his seat while viewing underwater features.

The impression of actually being part of the underwater scene becomes very real.

The boat's power source is so quiet it offers no distraction to the visitor.

It is possible to look a considerable distance laterally from the boat.

Some disadvantages are:

This is necessarily a "quiet water" boat.

To obtain interpretation, it is necessary to have an interpreter or some type cf device in the same compartment as the viewers, for the boat pilot cannot see what they are seeing, hence has little value as an interpreter. Even with an interpreter along, he finds it exceedingly difficult to serve all the people using the various portholes.

2. Other devices.

In Virgin Islands National Park, a self-guiding trail was developed for the scuba-equipped swimmer, the face mask and snorkel user, and those who wish to use the paddle board. This trail is laid out on the ocean floor in relatively shallow water. At key points of interest, an interpretive sign is securely anchored. It can be seen and read from beneath the water by swimmers using scuba equipment, or read from the surface through use of fins, face mask and snorkel, or using face mask and snorkel in combination with a paddle board.

In some areas, a rather small underwater viewing room has been constructed of concrete and equipped with a large plate glass window. Through this window the visitor can see whatever moves, or is located directly in front. This facility is effective for small numbers of visitors, but cannot handle many at a time. It does offer viewers an opportunity to do photography.

Underwater auditoriums have also come into use in some parts of the country. They require quiet water for installation. Two types of moveable and non-moveable ones are very effective:

The moveable type has large plate glass windows on one side of the structure, with seats facing the windows. The entire building can be moved, and tied securely in place at the desired location. Through an action somewhat similar to that of a submarine, sufficient water is let into compartments in the structure to gradually settle it deep enough to submerge the viewing windows. It is then held at this level, allowing visitors to walk onto the structure and down into the submerged auditorium, where wide views of the underwater world may be viewed at leisure. An interpreter explains the scene.

The non-moveable structure is solidly constructed on the shore of the water environment, but with its lower portion (the auditorium) extending several feet beneath the water surface. Large plate glass windows allow people in the auditorium to watch what takes place in front of them on the underwater "stage." An interpreter sits at a vantage point in the auditorium and explains the scene. This has proved a highly effective device. There are many underwater areas where such a facility might be used for interpretation of the natural scene.

Japan has developed underwater towers sitting off shore, along the ocean. The visitor is brought to the tower from shore by surface or cable craft. Inside he can visit viewing windows at more than one level.

That many other devices and methods could prove effective in underwater interpretation is a certainty. With fertile imagination we can expect vast strides in this field.

Top-Demonstrations for children showing how study skins are made for scientific collections, Boulder City Elementary School.

Left- Trail instruction, Hi Hill. Right- Showing the proper handling of reptiles, East Bay Regional Parks, California.

CHAPTER 8

Special Interpretive Programs

As might be expected, there are numerous interpretive programs that merit special consideration. Two in particular seem to warrant a somewhat detailed review: the program for children and the problem of meeting needs of the foreign visitor.

INTERPRETATION FOR CHILDREN

It is unfortunately true that children have often been overlooked in our interpretive programs. This is doubly unfortunate, because the child of today will be the citizen of tomorrow, and is by far the easiest to reach with your story. We have only to look at interpretive programs and activities of many areas to find that most efforts are directed toward the adult or near adult in age. Our museum exhibits tend to be too high above the floor for the child to see easily. Our illustrated talks are too often geared exclusively for adult audiences; and our conducted walks and other related activities are directed toward older members of the group. The child is also ignored in the texts of interpretive signs and roadside exhibits, and certainly in publications. Given one generation of children well indoctrinated in conservation and environmental values, and many of the nation's problems in those fields would be well on the way toward solution.

In trying to reach the young, we should strive for an age group between the 3rd and 7th grade levels in school. This is not saying younger or older children should be ignored, rather that this age group offers the best potential. Below the 3rd grade level a child's comprehension is not extensive, although his interest may be high. His interest span is still of rather short duration. Above the 7th grade, the youngster is adjusting to an adult world and adult thinking.

It is important to keep in mind that, while you may be dealing with a child, presentation of your subject should not be put in a little child's language.

By the time a youngster has reached the 3rd grade he uses and understands words that will often amaze you, and his level of comprehension is growing rapidly. Thus, don't talk to him as though he were a simple child, but as a young person who can very well understand what you are saying if you do not use too many complicated terms. Certainly there is feeling that one must "talk down" to young people of this type, but this is not necessary or desirable. Simply bring out your points in easily understood language.

The young person is especially easy to interest in natural history and ethnology. He has a natural interest in the animal world, and, of course, anything about Indians is certain to appeal.

A number of things should be considered in working with children on the trail, at an amphitheater, or in a museum situation. Some of the most important are:

Where possible, put your points across in story form. Telling about an incident involving an animal that you want the child to remember can be used to bring out characteristics of that animal. Children love stories, especially legends. Such stories as "Why the Coyote Howls," can easily be used to stimulate keen interest in early Indian life and culture.

Use human interest examples to put across important points. For instance, simply telling young people that feeding wild deer in the parks is detrimental to the animal does not carry nearly the "punch" that a true episode does; such as the account of the mother doe that was fed 13 candy bars in one morning by park visitors!

You must not expect every child to appear attentive, but he will likely know what is going on! Often some members of a group will seem to be occupied with anything except what you are trying to tell them. Don't be surprised, however, to learn that this seeming inattention is not real, and that they know very well what you have been saying.

Youngsters like to examine things to see how they work, act, etc. This natural curiosity should be utilized, specially in out-of-door situations where there is so much that can be shown. In museums, have things they can do, examine and make work. In such places as Yosemite National Park, Rock Creek Park in Washington, D C., and in several cities across the country, an entire museum is devoted to the young person and his interests. Here the youngster has the opportunity to use his senses of feel, sight, hearing and occasionally taste, to discover what something is and how it works.

The young person likes a sense of adventure. He likes to discover things. This can be encouraged and used to advantage, especially on trail, by challenging his powers of observation.

He likes to climb and squeeze into intriguing looking places. One or two such spots on a guided walk will be greeted with enthusiasm. Be sure, of course, that the spot chosen is safe.

The young person tends to be impatient, and wants to get along to the next point. Thus, care should be taken not to belabor a subject. If on trail, make stops relatively short and the interest points not too far apart.

A youngster likes to show the adult leader that he knows something about the subject. While care must be exercised that such "contributions" aren't too time consuming, still there is a real value in letting the child take an active part in the presentation.

If you can use a young person to demonstrate something to a group, do so if it is safe, and if the demonstration does not make the child the subject of ridicule.

Status is important to a young person, just as it is to you. He can be appealed to for order at a program or on a hike. Simple responsibilities, such as helping keep a group together on trail, gives him a sense of importance. However, discretion must be exercised in the amount of authority he is given to carry out his assignment.

In some areas, children's programs have been developed that are quite broad in scope and extend for periods of one to five days. Highly effective field trips are often the means of putting the chosen subject across. Museum exhibits and collections can be used where field trips are not possible. A suggested field program, covering a 3-day period and stressing the general subject of ecology, might be set up with these objectives:

To acquaint the child with a few of the basic concepts in nature that can be readily seen and understood.

To acquaint the child with conservation as practiced by the agency or area.

To give each child a chance to enrich his knowledge of nature with an interesting out-door experience.

For this program, it is believed that children should be not less than 8 years of age and normally not more than 12. Below the age of 8 the attention span is too limited and comprehension is not sufficiently high. Above 12, the youngster is a teenager and much aware of the fact. He, or she, with other teenagers, tends to isolate from the group, and thus the leader has in reality two groups with divergent interests. Those above 12 years should be encouraged to join a conducted trip with an adult group. While not usually encouraged to do so, parents should feel free to accompany their children on activities of the group. Actually they get as much enjoyment out of these activities as do the children.

Operation of the field program is not complicated. Instruction is carried out along the trail. At the beginning of each walk it is helpful to collect the group and briefly state the story or activity to be covered, such as "Today we are going to learn something of the story of rocks; how mountains and canyons are made." Discuss the importance of being a good observer. Point out that "everything has a story" if the observer is sharp enough to see it. Stress that each one will know some part of the story, and when each has put his knowledge together with others in the group, the story will be complete. Stress the importance of not trampling vegetation, staying together, etc.

This is to be an experience in which lasting impressions and truths are gained and learned. Because this is true, it is important that "telling" by the leader be kept at a much reduced level. Instead, encourage the individual members of the group to help develop the story. Ask leading questions. Should the leader get a "wrong answer," it cannot be ignored or belittled. Without too much difficulty, however, the leader can take the wrong answer and find application in some phase of the morning's activities. Present points that have quite apparent relationships, so that details of the story can be supplied by the individual; fill in facts only where it isn't likely the group will know them. This is in a way a game of "detective." The leader helps locate the clues, and individual members of the group have the thrill of putting newly discovered clues together to tell a story. It is no great problem to present stories in nature, as clues are many and easy to see. Always stress the use of the five senses. Most children (and adults) depend upon hearing and seeing, but seldom use the senses of touch, taste and smell. A feature in nature acquires distinct character when experienced by as many of the senses as are possible to use. This field experience, if well done, leaves the child with a sense of having contributed, of taking part. It is *his* trip as well as the leader's. Because of this, he is a ready recipient of any ideas the leader wishes to introduce.

Materials to be covered in the program should be basically simple, and used to demonstrate general concepts. These concepts must be easily recognized, of general application, and capable of being demonstrated with numerous on-site examples. The following general concepts are suggested:

a. There is constant change on the earth.

This is simple and easily demonstrated. Here is found the story of rocks, mountain building, erosion, weathering, temperature, climate, etc. This is the story of landscape and what happens to it.

b. Plants and animals influence change on the earth.

Here are told the many ways in which both plants and animals contribute to topography. The stories of watersheds, formation of soils, erosion control, fire control, relationship of plants to slope and temperature, the work of animals, etc., are among those that can be demonstrated.

c. Plants and animals relate to each other.

Here can be shown the hundreds of stories of how each form of plant and animal life contribute to the existence and well being of other biological forms.

Duration time for field trips should normally not exceed 2½ hours for each trip made. All interpretation should be carried out on trail or in areas where excessive damage will not be caused by a conventional walk away from a designated trail. Each day's program should be designed to cover, in detail, the primary concept assigned to that day. Subjects handled from day to day should lead naturally from one concept to another and back again. A child having only one day will grasp the application of all three concepts, and have a really broad understanding of at least one.

The above is only one suggested program for children. There are many others, of course. You, as the interpreter, will need only to select the subject you want to use, and then work out a systematic way to approach it. Certainly the value of such a program to the child cannot be clearly understood until you have actually presented one. Then you will know!

Children under twelve are much like modeling clay. They can be molded into a desired pattern with a minimum of effort. To work with them and watch their minds unfold is a most rewarding experience for the genuine interpreter.

INTERPRETATION FOR FOREIGN VISITORS

Some years ago, while on a guided hike to the top of Yosemite Falls in Yosemite National Park, a very earnest young man was trying to follow what the naturalist in charge of the trip was saying. Finally, in complete frustration, he exclaimed out loud, "I wish there were someone who could tell me what he is saying!" Now this didn't sound so much out of the ordinary—except that the man spoke in French. As sometimes happens, one member of the party knew a little French, and spoke to the man. Immediately there was a flurry of questions, somewhat awkwardly answered in uncertain French. However, the two stayed together all day, and the trip ended with a very grateful foreigner trying to express his appreciation for the assistance received.

Now this incident is not a rarity. Perhaps the French visitor didn't get all the help he wanted, but he was there, wishing someone could help him. The numbers of his kind have been steadily increasing through the years, and today we have large numbers visiting this country. Some understand and speak English; many do not.

This is an aspect of interpretation too often overlooked. We see the foreigner around, but we really don't know what he is getting in the way of help, and we have nothing especially set up for him in our interpretive programs. This is important, as he is getting an impression of our country, and we could help so very much to make it a good one. He will appreciate any effort we make, as it tells him we recognize his existence.

What we can do for this visitor depends in large measure on where he calls home. He may speak English very well (many do), in which case there is no great language barrier to overcome. He can visit our great parks and forests, historical buildings and other objects of interest, and pretty well get along on his own. He may be over here on government business, in which case he may need no guidance. He may be a student, especially interested in seeing our country and learning more of how we live.

Foreign visitors like to do many things. Many like to take pictures, and there are no shutter-bugs as ardent as the Japanese. Many enjoy hiking, and our high mountains attract groups from Germany, Norway and Sweden in large numbers. They like to climb to heights, but are not necessarily mountain climbers. They like to hear interesting stories of local color, especially if they pertain to the West. Some are interested in history of one type or another, especially if it has been made by people from their country. They like to collect pictures, folders and some souvenirs.

What can the interpreter do for them? There are definitely some things to do and some things not to do. Some of these are:

Try to remember a name if given to you. This is important to him. Watch and listen to how he pronounces it; he will be complimented if you say it right.

Go out of your way a bit to help his understanding of what you are showing him.

Be a good listener. Try to understand him and his needs. This allows you to assist him information-wise.

If he can understand you, be sure of word selection that will help make your meaning clear.

Speak somewhat deliberately. He may not be able to follow if you speak rapidly, and may miss your real meaning.

Try to speak in terms of his interest, if you can.

Compare what he sees to things you know are in his country, but do not belittle in these comparisons.

Do *not* talk politics, race, religion or become involved in such. Don't "point with pride" about things American in too positive a way; it may sound boastful to him.

Put up bulletin boards where they will be seen by most foreign visitors with information on them in some of the most commonly used languages.

Put out foreign language booklets or leaflets. Some parks and airlines do this, especially on safety instructions.

Put up elevation signs showing heights in meters as well as feet.

Investigate possibilities of on-site tape repeaters, with the message given in several languages. There are machines from which the chosen language can be heard by simply pushing a selector button.

If you are in an area where a certain foreign language is commonly encountered, such as Spanish in the southern portions of our country, try to hire bilingual help. Also, check your local staff, it is sometimes surprising how many may know a foreign language and can be of real assistance.

One word of caution. In this country we often find it helpful to cater a bit to children. However, it is best to be a bit careful in admiring youngsters who are part of a foreign group. Mothers not acquainted with our free and easy way of talking to anyone may incorrectly interpret your attention. Be very careful about touching a foreign child—in some countries this is simply not tolerated.

Much can be done for the foreign visitor. It takes only an appreciation of his problems, and a realization that he is definitely in your group because he wants to learn something. All interpretive programs should take him into consideration.

Top-Tumacacori National Monument. Lower Left-Visitor Center, Aztec National Monument.

CHAPTER 9

The Visitor Center or Museum

The interpretive program can center in a variety of facilities or activities, but is usually located in a visitor center, museum or similar structure. It is here that the primary story of an area or featured subject is presented in some detail to the visitor. Several interpretive activities may originate in or from this facility. It is usually headquarters for the interpretive staff. Most important of all, it is here that the visitor comes in contact with the total program, and can select those activities in which he wishes to take part.

Location of the facility is a most important factor. Where possible, it should be near the visitor's normal route of travel as he enters the area. This enables his first stop at a point where he can get the most assistance in planning his time. Here he will find the key stories of the area, each of which should be designed to be told quickly and clearly. Design of the building is, of course, the job of the architect, but the interpreter can often offer valuable suggestions regarding such things as the lobby, location and design of the information desk, and ways in which the exhibit, audiovisual and work rooms are to be used. An exhibit plan for the building is a subject apart from this discussion. Seldom is the interpreter talented in display techniques. His job is to outline the stories to be told, and let the exhibit designer work out details.

The interpreter is concerned, however, with such things as the information desk and its operation, the audiovisual programs (if any), and any reference collections and their uses.

It is the person at the information desk who helps set the tone for the visitor. Its operation is one of the most important functions of the interpretive program, and one of the most difficult to do well. The attitude of the visitor brings to the desk is largely out of the interpreter's hands. It may be good or bad. However, the attitude he takes away is the responsibility of the interpreter. Thus, one of the first things that must be considered is the impression the visitor receives. Four main factors do much to create a favorable or unfavorable impression:

1. The attitude the visitor brings with him.

This is difficult to gauge in the few seconds as he approaches the information desk. He may have had a bad experience before entering the building that may show itself in any number of ways—discourteous, grouchy, sarcastic, rude, or demanding. On the contrary he may make the job of the interpreter easy by displaying a smile, friendliness and interest. Whatever his attitude may be, the job of the desk attendant is to send him away in a good frame of mind.

2. The appearance of the desk attendant.

A good appearance doesn't solve all the problems that may come to the desk, but it goes a long way toward it! Nothing will cause the visitor to become non-receptive quicker than to find the desk attendant sloppy in appearance. A droopy shirt, soiled neck-tie, uncombed hair, dirty finger nails, too much make-up, and a "tired slouch" will go far toward driving the visitor away, both mentally and physically.

3. The appearance of the desk and its surroundings.

The desk should always appear neat and well organized. Everything should have a place and be in it.

**Information
Center, Chaco Canyon.**

4. The attitude of the attendant.

Even though the first three items above have been taken care of, the attendant can still insure a negative encounter by a poor approach. If the attendant is courteous, patient, cheerful, and quite obviously proud of his job, the chances are the visitor will respond in the desired manner.

There are several things that can be of assistance to the information desk attendant. Good maps are important, if the area being visited is very extensive. These should always be readily available, but not put out on the counter for everyone to help himself. The supply will melt rapidly if this is done, as everyone from age 5 to 50 will take one, regardless of how many are in one family. A map of the area, mounted under glass for everyone to see, is most helpful. It should have key routes and trails in color. A large wall map behind the desk, in three dimension if possible, is very useful. The desk should be well lighted, so that all visitors can see easily. Not everyone will have eyesight adapted to dim light. If properly designed, any programs in the audiovisual room can be activated from the desk by the attendant.

There will always be problems to solve; some easy, others not so. Questions will always be many and varied. They will range from "where are the rest rooms?" to "what is the name of the gray bird I saw down the road?" In every case it is the desk attendant who must handle the question tactfully and helpfully. He must keep in mind that it is never a silly question being asked. The visitor is simply wanting to know something that is, at the moment at least, important to him. A question is silly only when asked in a manner that obviously is used for effect.

There is always the problem of children (and some adults) who do not realize that others would appreciate less noise. To get a child to reduce his lung output without antagonizing parents calls for real tact. There is always the visitor who likes to engage the desk attendant in conversation and monopolize all his attention. Again, tact is required to resolve the matter. If the attendant is a girl, there is always the young man (or much older!) who likes to impress her, and makes it difficult for her to do her job. There is also the person who wants to tell the attendant what is wrong with the operation of the area, museum or facility.

The information desk, if properly operated, sets the stage for an enjoyable visitor experience. While the opportunity for interpretation tends to be somewhat limited, an interested and knowledgeable attendant can steer the visitor into activities that will give him a better appreciation of the values of the area.

Many visitor centers and museums have a room set aside to house all reference collections. These will vary from area to area. Some have extensive collections; others will have only limited materials. The value of a collection is measured in its usefulness, not its size. In a general museum, the collections may range over a broad assortment of items covering many subjects. In a visitor center they should be pretty much restricted to the area, or closely related to some important story in the nearby region.

Large unplanned collections are almost useless for study and research. The care of such collections is wasteful of staff time, and usually at the expense of more valuable specimens. They occupy space, causing crowding which can do damage.

In helping build up reference collections, the interpreter should:

Be concerned with having an inventory of the important area fauna and flora, rocks and minerals, historical and archeological objects, or other subjects of value to the interpretive program.

Be concerned with any rare specimens, as he may not be able to obtain them again.

Collect only what is required, and not load up on some subject simply because of personal interest.

Be concerned with items of special interest to visitors.

Interior diorama of Father Kino location.

Collect any oddities of scientific interest. Have a place for these, but just building up a collection of "freaks" is not sound.

Have a reference series ranging from the common to the uncommon. There is a tendency to ignore the common simply because it is. Common things have a habit of becoming uncommon with the passage of time.

The value of a really good reference collection to the interpreter is often overlooked, and thus many valuable materials are not available when needed. Such a collection:

Is of use to show interested scientists and students.

Is a source of reference for publications that are planned or being developed.

Is a constant source of reference for talks, hikes, etc.

Is a source of identification for the many things visitors are always bringing to you.

Gives stature to your program in the mind of the visitor.

Teaches the value of careful, systematic work to your staff.

Is of interest to visitors. For example, a bird collection can be most helpful to those who have been on a bird walk and wish to delve into the subject a bit deeper. Where possible, a collection should also include hand specimens.

However you may choose to use the facilities, exhibits, audio-visual devices, reference collections, etc., in the visitor center or museum, you have at your command most useful and helpful aids in giving your program a strong flavor of quality so important to the visitor.

Campfire Circle.

CHAPTER 10

Campfire Circles and Amphitheaters

Because of their importance to the interpreter, the campfire circle and amphitheater warrant special consideration in developing and operating an interpretive program. To the visitor, the evening program is often a "must" part of his visit to a park or similar area. Here he has opportunity to learn more about the area, its natural history, history and other values. Here also he can meet the interpreter and get questions answered on many subjects.

Such a facility will be found useful in several ways. Of course the evening program is basic. However, it also serves as an excellent meeting place to start conducted walks. It offers a place for the first comers to sit down while waiting for the walk to begin. When special groups visit an area it is a good place to hold meetings, and to collect tour members for briefing.

Because they are both similar and dissimilar in many respects, let us examine each facility separately.

THE CAMPFIRE CIRCLE

The campfire circle has an appeal that is difficult to evaluate. Something about sitting around a campfire in an under-the-stars situation makes a lasting impression on people. No other activity is quite the same.

Location of the circle is of considerable importance. It must not be difficult to reach on foot, and must be far enough from roads and parking areas that traffic noises are not a factor. Car noises and headlights can be real problems. The road approach, if one is planned, should be so designed that car headlights from late arrivals do not swing across the circle, as this is very distracting to both the speaker and the audience. Acoustics should be considered. If possible, a background of trees or a rocky wall make it easier for the speaker to be heard. Such also serves as a windbreak. The fire pit should be somewhat to one side or other from where the speaker is to stand. If this is not done, the audience has to look toward the fire and can see only a silhouette of the speaker during the program.

Advantages of a campfire circle include:

An informal atmosphere. Here can develop a feeling of group intimacy that is often difficult to achieve in larger, more formal facilities.

Seating is usually less formal than in the amphitheater or indoor auditorium. The seats are normally rustic in character (logs, etc.) arranged in a semi-circle, and allow for "elbow" contact with other visitors. This becomes important if singing is part of the program.

The visitor is reasonably close to the campfire, which has great appeal. Almost everyone likes to watch the fire as the program is getting ready to begin. Because the setting is informal, the speaker finds he is much more "accessible" to the visitors before the program begins and after it ends.

Visitors enjoy standing around the fire for a short time after the program is over. This gives the speaker an opportunity to meet several of them.

The facility is economical to install and maintain. It can be altered without difficulty should the need arise.

There are, of course, some obvious disadvantages:

Usually the speaker has no electricity available, and must present his program without projectors and other visual aids requiring electrical power. He has to rely primarily upon his ability to communicate.

Lack of visual facilities restricts the subject matter the speaker can use.

The speaker is greatly restricted in showing hand-held objects because of inadequate light.

Usually there is no sound amplification, although several good, portable, battery operated sound systems can be obtained.

Because electric lighting is not usually available, care must be taken to prevent visitor exposure to possible injury when darkness comes.

THE AMPHITHEATER

This is a much more involved facility, tantamount to moving a large auditorium out-of-doors, but without the ceiling and walls. Otherwise the physical makeup is quite similar. Because of its size and seating arrangement, the atmosphere is much more formal, even though the interpreter may strive to present a relaxed program.

Location is very important. Because it is designed to handle large numbers of people, the amphitheater must be easily accessible to be successful. This means it must be within easy walking distance of a parking area, as many people will want to come in cars, especially older persons who may not be able to walk very far. However, the parking area (or areas) must be located so that car noises do not hinder presentation of the program, and their headlights do not swing across the audience and hit the projection screen. As with the campfire circle, the matter of acoustics should be considered, although a properly installed sound system will remedy most acoustical defects arising from location. Natural screening by trees and other plants can help solve the matter of acoustics and the twin problems of traffic noises and lights.

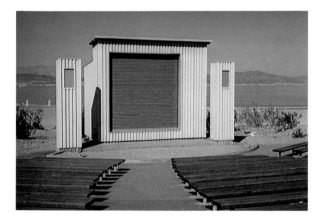

**Amphitheater with rear
screen unit, Boulder Beach,
Lake Mead.**

Amphitheater design requires consideration of several factors. Among the most important are:

1. The stage building.

This structure can be designed for either rear or front screen projection. If rear screen, the building behind the screen serves as the projection room, and furnishes general storage and utility space as well. Sound equipment and tape decks are also located here. If front screen projection is used, only storage and utility space is usually made a part of the building.

The floor of the stage should be about two feet above ground level. Opinions vary, but this height has proven very effective. This places the speaker high enough above the audience for him to see everyone, and for them to see him. The stage should be longer than the projection screen is wide to allow space at either side for the speaker and the picture at the same time.

Size of the screen will vary with seating capacity. The larger the audience, the larger the screen will need to be. Generally a 12' × 12' screen is effective with an audience of 500 or more. Smaller sizes will give good results for smaller groups. A rear screen unit should have a roller type door, power operated, coming down over the screen when not in use to give it vital protection. For front screen projection the screen may either be a large roll-down type or a painted surface. If the latter, a roller door is highly desirable to protect against weather and vandalism. If a roll-down screen is used, no protective door is needed, but the screen box should be under a protective "roof" to keep out rain, snow or dirt. Roll-down screens require care that moths, etc., are not rolled up in them after a program is completed.

All projection and sound equipment are to be located inside the same building if a rear screen unit is used. With front screen projection, these items will be in the projection building. Equipment should include amplifiers, tape decks, and both slide and movie projectors. Speakers for the sound system are usually quite effective if mounted one on either side of the screen and high enough above the stage floor to discourage vandalism. Column speakers appear more effective than other types. The microphone (or microphones) on stage should be transmitter or necklace type, with a long cord. Either kind eliminates the need to carry a hand mike, or operate from behind a microphone stand, thus giving the speaker more mobility and free hands for other things.

There should be a control panel at one side of the screen, set into the wall and so designed that it can be securely locked. Inside should be switches and controls for all the lights, projectors, amplifiers, power outlets, etc. This enables the MC or speaker to control the entire program from on stage. By turning on amplifiers for all equipment to be used at the start of the program, he can use any sound or projection unit desired at the flick of a switch. Do *not* put power outlets outside of the panel box. Often these outlets are placed along the front of the stage—perfect locations for filling them with chewing gum, sticks and the like! The control box can also be designed large enough to house a small flashlight-type arrow pointer, which is thus readily available should the speaker need to indicate something being shown on the screen.

2. The fire pit.

Many amphitheaters are built with a fire pit. This is normally used prior to commencement of the regular evening program. Its location is important. It should be to one side or the other of the stage building, and several feet away from the stage. It should be placed far enough forward so light from the fire will have minimal effect upon the screen. This is essential, as the "campfire," once it is burning well, may not burn down enough by the time the projection screen is to be used, and may reduce effectiveness of the picture image. Or, as often happens, some helpful visitors may add fuel to the fire while the program is in progress. As a side note on this possibility, *never* have more fuel at the fire pit than you expect to use!

3. The amphitheater seats.

Make these as comfortable as you can. Often the argument is heard that seats with comfortable back rests are not in harmony with the natural scene in which the amphitheater may be located. No doubt this is true, but neither is the stage building, the screen, the sound systems, or even the presence of the seats themselves! As an interpreter you have the task of putting your story across to audiences running into the hundreds of people, and the job becomes a bit difficult to accomplish if they begin to suffer from poorly designed seats and aching backs.

4. Front screen projection booth.

If front screen projection is used, the booth should house all equipment. The projection window should be high enough above the ground that late comers to the program will not interfere with the picture being shown on the screen. This problem can also be helped by having an aisle from the booth to the stage, thus tending to eliminate the urge some people have to stand on a seat and make "finger images" on the screen when the projector is in use.

5. Area lights.

By all means, there should be ground lights to illuminate walkways, and subdued ground lights located on the aisles to help the late comer see where he is going. Good overhead lights at strategic points around the outside of the amphitheater, for use before and after a program, are a must.

An amphitheater with the above basic elements will allow the interpreter to devote his attention to the task at hand, and give his program the professional touch it needs to be successful.

CHAPTER 11

Audio and Audio Visual Devices

The use of electronic devices in interpretation can be extremely helpful, and goes far toward presenting a well balanced program. There is no real substitute for the interpreter in guided activities and presentation of talks. However, the tape recorder, tape repeater, slide-tape show, and motion picture film can render most valuable assistance. In recent years, the use of radio and television offer additional tools to the imaginative interpreter.

Because these devices are of considerable importance, let us review some of the ways in which they are most valuable.

THE TAPE RECORDER

Not every agency or area can finance full scale audiovisual presentation. For those who must begin in a modest way, the tape recorder can contribute a great deal, and lay the foundation for more sophisticated programs as money becomes available.

Most tape recorders, including the cassette type, can be purchased for a reasonable sum. Once you have one, several ways in which it can be used are at your command. You are limited only by your imagination. However, the following should be helpful:

1. For recording talks.

The recorder is one of the best aids available in helping to train your staff, and yourself, in the skill of giving talks before audiences. There is nothing more revealing than to "dry run" a talk with a recorder and see how you sound. Weaknesses in presentation and organization become obvious as the talk is played back. Often you will find that you have over-used certain words, and that some are not pronounced right or enunciated clearly. Certain speech mannerisms will likely show up. Tone of voice and rate of speaking are faithfully reproduced for your evaluation. If you have one or more interpretive staff members, especially seasonal help, a recording of campfire, amphitheater or auditorium presentations furnishes the best possible basis for review.

2. For reference library.

Often a speaker develops an outstanding program on a subject that would be valuable as reference material or as an aid to other speakers who plan to speak on the same, or closely related, subject. Seasonal help find it most valuable, in preparing a talk, to hear tape recordings of other successful speakers and see how they handled the subject. Most really good talks are well researched, to be sure that all data used are accurate. Thus, the recording will include much reliable information that might not be known to the listener. Such tapes should be catalogued and retained in a library just as any book might be.

3. The taped interview.

There are many reasons why the interpreter should become proficient in carrying out a taped interview. Among them are:

It is valuable as a means of recording "dying" history. People get old, and too often their experiences die with them. Putting memorable events on tape as an early day resident of an area remembers them, recording reminiscences of an older naturalist, archeologist, etc., or recording old time folk tales, are examples of material that can easily be lost for all time. This writer recalls hearing an old timer relate his experiences with grizzly bears and how they reacted to early day hunters and trappers in the late 1800's. The stories were fascinating, but there was no tape recorder at that time! Valuable information was lost. One word of caution: When the interview is to be used as historical reference, never edit the recording by cutting it. Leave it "as is," in proper context. Re-record any sections you may need to use.

The recorder enables the interpreter to preserve voices of important personalities for posterity.

When a person is being interviewed, he will often relate more about himself or his experiences than if he were writing it.

The interview can sometimes be used as a "dub in" for movies or sound script, especially short sections of it. Permission to do so should be obtained first, however.

Here are some valuable techniques to use in interviewing:

Be sure the person being interviewed is comfortable before you begin.

Remember he is the one being interviewed. Direct the conversation through your questions or comments, but let him do the talking.

By all means get him to relax prior to the time for actual recording. If not, allow the interview to pass the "loosening up" stage before getting into detailed specifics.

A lapel or necklace microphone is usually better than one held in the hand or set on a table. He may be a bit overawed at sight of a mike, and the lapel mike is small and unobtrusive.

It is important that the interviewer be familiar enough with the subject under discussion to ask good questions. This may not always be possible, as the person being interviewed may be pulling on his past experience. Thus, the interviewer must be constantly alert to improvise, based on his own knowledge and background. This can usually be accomplished.

Usually the interview comes easy if you center the opening remarks on things that are likely close to him, such as his home, family, etc.

Avoid asking questions that can be answered with a "yes" or "no."

Ask any formal or technical questions only after the interview has progressed a few minutes. By this time he is as relaxed as he will ever be.

Be ready to close out at any time that he may seem tired or ready to quit. Nothing is more deadly than an obviously reluctant interviewee.

Record the date, place and name of the person speaking. This can either be placed at the beginning of the interview or after it has terminated. Sometimes it is best to record it after the interview is over, and at a later time insert the recording at the beginning of the tape. This tends to eliminate one element of formality in the interview.

You might find it helpful to check your performance as an interviewer against the following:

Were you friendly?
Did the interviewee respond to your friendliness?
Were you interested in him as an individual?
Were you interested in his remarks?
Were you unhurried and relaxed?
Did you prepare adequately for the interview?
Did he seem at ease?
Did you try to reduce his nervousness or fear?
Did you get him to tell what was on his mind?
Did you give him enough time to talk?
Did you disagree with him verbally at any time?
Did you ask questions that were challenging or argumentative?
Did you listen to everything he said, or did you simply hear?
Did you encourage him to give examples or to elaborate on unclear points?
Did you close on a friendly note?

There are other uses for the recorder. It can be used in making tapes for exhibits, both for use indoors and for on-site. The portable recorder—the cassette type—can be used on guided walks to take along recorded sounds or narrative that you want your group to hear. Bird calls can be put on tape and taken into the field for playback at the appropriate time should the live birds fail to cooperate! Statements by well known personalities about an historic or archeological site, etc., can be used at selected places.

THE TAPE REPEATER

This device is usually associated with sites where you lack the manpower to do the job. It can be equally effective on self-guiding trails. At one time it was not possible to have repeaters on a trail due to lack of power, but this is no longer true, for good battery driven devices are now available. Some use underground cables from a source of power. Most repeaters are not completely all-weather devices, but are largely so.

There are several very definite values to the repeater:

It is very useful where the message is rather lengthy.

The human voice helps attract and hold visitor attention.

People like to activate things, and especially to push buttons.

There is always curiosity to see what the repeater has to say.

It is especially useful in historical and archeological areas. It is in character in such a setting. The voice is not out of place, and can impart drama to the text. Also, drama can be accentuated by sound, such as bugle calls, etc.

The installation and maintenance costs are not high.

As part of an exhibit, it can be changed without great expense.

Naturally there are some undesirable aspects to a device of this type:

Care must be exercised in choosing where it is to be used. In many out-of-door situations, especially in a wilderness atmosphere, it can be entirely out of character.

It can be an intrusion and an irritant. Definitely it does not add to the inspirational and aesthetic impact of a great scenic view. Not everyone wants to hear a voice at such a moment.

It is subject to vandalism and mischief makers. A pin jammed in by the side of the push button can cause lots of trouble!

It requires some maintenance and replacement. Temperature changes may adversely affect its operation.

Writing the message for the tape repeater is not a simple task. It requires considerable thought as to what you want to say and to whom your message is directed. Duration time is very important. Most messages should not exceed three minutes in length, and shorter ones are usually desirable. The location of the repeater has an important bearing on the message, as people tire rather quickly. If the visitor has to stand up while listening to the message, he will want to move sooner than if he is seated.

The repeater message is not just a vocal interpretive sign; it is basically a short talk. Many of the elements to be considered in presenting a non-illustrated talk must be utilized (see Chapter 4). The voice of the narrator must carry the full load, as few aids can be used. In some instances, sound can be dubbed in for background (such as the sound of cannon, voices, wind, etc.), but for the most part the narrator's voice is the central feature. The importance of word selection must be carefully considered. Even good speakers may have difficulty with some sounds; thus special care should be taken not to load the script with words containing the letter "s," as such tends to produce hissing sounds over a microphone.

Three items are basic in writing the message:

It must have an arresting opening. The first few words will either catch the listener's attention, or he will drift on to something else without hearing the entire message. Don't be hammy, but do get his attention!

There must be a quick, meaty story following closely on the heels of your attention-getting opening sentences. This is the reason for the repeater being used at this particular location.

The message should close out with a punch thought or sentence. Don't just come to the end and stop! Leave the listener with a feeling that this message was stimulating; that the subject is worthy of a follow-up. Your objective is to get immediate action on the part of the listener.

The tape repeater can be used in so many situations that its value as an interpretive aid cannot be minimized. When the actual interpreter cannot be had, it is a valuable and effective substitute.

THE SLIDE-TAPE PROGRAM

Joining together of the tape recorder and the slide projector under electronic controls is a popular and effective device for short length programs designed primarily for audiovisual room and auditorium use. Its operation is simple. At the push of a button, the electronic controls start the tape, slowly lower the room lights, and turn on the projector. The program then proceeds, with electronic impulses on the tape controlling the change of slides. As the program ends, the lights are slowly brought up again, the taped message is terminated, and the equipment recycles itself, ready to start over again. It is then shut off by the electronic control. Nothing could be easier to do!

There are several basic values to such a device. Some of these are:

It offers the interpretive program considerable latitude and flexibility in subject matter, ranging from simple orientation to more complex subjects.

It serves efficiently where manpower cannot be committed to short, illustrated talks.

It can be operated by the information desk receptionist or other attendant without on the spot supervision. The simple pushing of a button does the entire job.

There are some negative factors that go with it:

It requires careful handling, as it is not damage proof.

It requires good preventative maintenance, which is a matter of constant concern.

Initial cost of the various elements in the equipment is not cheap. However, the machine should last a long time with good care.

Slides must be constantly checked for projection quality. There is always a tendency to overlook gradual loss of color values in a slide, and such things as scratches, dirt and cracked glass on bound slides are often not conscientiously corrected.

Tapes eventually wear, impairing quality of the sound, and must be replaced.

Preparation of script is of prime importance. Basically it must be what you would present on a thoughtfully worded, well illustrated program. There should be good story continuity, tied in closely with the visual material. Simple language should be used, with a minimum of technical terms. There is no time in this type of program to go into an explanation of unfamiliar terms. Slides should come on at somewhat regular intervals, and should be the backdrop for what the tape is saying. Don't write a program about the slides; use the slides to illustrate your story. Normally a slide should not stay on the screen for more than 15–20 seconds, although at times a longer period is necessary. Don't change slides too fast. Likely you will want music to introduce and end the program, but do not have it too loud.

MOVIES

Little need be said about the value of movies, except that some-times there is a tendency to seek film presentations for the major part of the interpretive effort. Again, it should be recognized that a film cannot take the place of the interpreter himself. A film is static, with little change possible to reflect new knowledge. It is not cheap to buy, and is expensive to produce. All too often the film you find available does not really show what you want. Film maintenance and replacement is a matter of constant concern. Several good manuals are available on the care and operation of projection equipment, so no effort will be made here to explain the steps that should be taken to insure good projection and longer life for films.

With all its problems, movie film offers one of the most universally accepted media for the interpreter's use.

RADIO

It is unfortunately true that this excellent device is too often overlooked by interpreters. We give talks before clubs and or-ganizations, and work with school groups, but radio is seldom used. Yet this is one of the most effective devices available, and allows your interpretive message to reach scores of people who would likely not hear it otherwise. Possibly the non-use of radio stems from a feeling that one must be a professional at the game in order to produce a good program; or, there is very often real reluctance to use a microphone. The thought of talking to an unseen audience actually scares many a person who wouldn't hesitate to address a visible audience.

A radio station is a fertile field for good, short programs. Every station manager is on the lookout for material that he thinks may interest his listening public. The stories you have to tell are also designed to interest this same listening public. The only problem is how to put the two items together.

Actually it is usually not too much of a problem, and the cost of producing such programs is minimal. All you need is a good tape recorder (not a cassette), and a quiet room with good acoustics in which to make a recording. The program should normally be designed to last about 12–12½ minutes, as this allows for the time required by the station announcer to introduce the program, make any necessary announcements, and close it out in the 15 minutes usually made available by the station. Check first to be sure of the preferred program length.

Three types of programs are easy to prepare and present. Not all are "live," in that they are put on tape for sending to the radio station. One is the interview type in which someone is interviewed on a subject of interpretive value. It is an off-the-cuff, unrehearsed show. Another is the round table discussion involving two or more persons in which one acts as the moderator. He directs the flow of the discussion and poses thoughts for the others to clarify. It is also unrehearsed, although the participants know what subjects will be discussed. A variation of this is the "open end" program in which you do not necessarily come to the end of the subject, but simply pick up the thread of it on the next program. This is especially effective when developing a series of programs on some subject. The third involves one or more persons in which a prepared script is followed. This does not allow for deviation.

A number of points should be considered when making either the interview or round table programs:

Don't try to cover too much territory. You have only a limited amount of time available, and much time will be taken up in comments or thoughts, personal experiences, etc., by the participants. Usually 3 to 5 items are about all you can handle effectively in one program.

Keep some material in reserve to discuss just in case things move along more rapidly than anticipated, but don't cut off a good discussion too soon.

Personal experiences are fine, but don't use "I" too much. Your listening audience will likely not appreciate it.

Don't try to be funny. Good spontaneous humor, obviously not planted, is good, but humorous attempts may sound pretty flat on radio where the voice is everything.

Don't forget that your audience is largely local listeners. Use good, interesting stories, local in nature, to tie your interpretive story together.

Be relaxed. This may not be easy for some, but the listener can usually sense when the conversation is forced. Keep in mind that you can always redo the tape if you make a mistake.

Don't talk too close to the microphone, for hisses may be produced. Usually about 10–12 inches is a good distance. Placing the microphone on a small table between participants on the program allows everyone to be recorded clearly and with proper volume. Necklace or lapel microphones and a "mixer" capable of taking care of them is by far the best arrangement, however.

If by some chance you are running your program outside where wind is a factor, a handkerchief tied over the microphone will eliminate the rumble of the wind going over the instrument.

Written notes can be most helpful for reference. These should be in proper sequence for presentation.

While the most effective types of programs by the non-professional are the interview and round table discussions, there are times when a script is necessary. In fact, some radio stations prefer it. This type of program may place you entirely on your own, or you may use other persons. However, the more persons involved in a formal script, the more care must be taken, and usually some rehearsals are desirable. If by yourself, you have to realize that *you are* the program and cannot rely on anyone else. The program resolves itself into how to properly read what you have written, and in a conversational tone so that the result does not sound stilted.

Some points worth remembering are:

The projection of your personality is a must.

Be sure you read easily and not too fast. You can record again, if necessary, unless on a "live" show.

Watch the rustling of papers as you shift from one page to another. Usually it is helpful to fan out the pages you are holding for ease of selection. Then you simply let the discarded page drop noiselessly onto the table or floor.

Watch a tendency to hesitate as you shift from one page to another.

Watch the tendency to sigh as you read. Often the reader isn't aware that he does this.

Watch modulation; your tone of voice must have life in it.

Speak distinctly and not too fast. This helps eliminate hisses. Often there is a tendency to speed up as the program proceeds.

Writing a radio script for programs of this type is similar in technique to that of a good repeater tape message. With good knowledge of your own subject and how you want to present it, you really have the three basics to again consider:

Have a strong opening statement.

Follow with a well-rounded discussion, interspersed with examples and experiences.

Have a punch close out. In this you are not trying to achieve immediate action on the part of the listener, as is done with a repeater tape message; you are merely trying to develop a desire to do so.

A radio station is required to devote a portion of its broadcast time to public service programs. The interpretive program, if well done, can often find a station manager quite willing to give it air time.

TELEVISION

This is naturally an excellent interpretive device if an occasion arises where it can be used. However, unlike radio, there is little if any free time made available by a television station. Techniques vary in developing programs of this nature, so no attempt will be made to suggest what might be the best procedures. This is a specialized field.

Developing New Ideas

CHAPTER 12

Looking Ahead

Since the beginning of planned interpretive programs in various parks, forests, museums, and related facilities, many ideas have been advanced to improve their quality and effectiveness. Several of these we still have; others have been discarded for failure to produce desired results. There is little doubt that some of the methods, techniques and devices of today will also be superseded by tomorrow's developments. Thus, it is essential that each interpreter have an open mind, and be constantly on the alert to use ideas as they come along.

New ideas and devices may show up almost anywhere. A visit to a large public display, such as a world's fair, will usually uncover several thought-provoking ideas that, with minor modifications or no changes at all, are worth trying out in your program. For example, at one such fair, Eastman Kodak came up with a simple device for using color projection in out-of-door exhibits; a technique that had not been used before. A museum is also a fertile field for ideas on display, especially if it is a modern, progressive type of facility. However, if you are to have a constantly improving program, you cannot afford to sit and wait for someone else to come up with new ideas and improvements. Try some of your own; they might prove successful!

There are some fields where we can surely anticipate innovations, and we should watch them with more than casual interest. Among these are:

The use of car radios and on-site transmitters. Radio frequencies can now be worked out, and such a device has been very successfully utilized for guided tours.

The use of cassette tapes in cars and on self-guided tours. Several kinds of self-guidance using this device are being successfully used here and there.

The use of videotape. With portable video equipment now in use, interpretive programs can be made and viewed in an auditorium the same day.

The use of closed-circuit television. Here are many possibilities. In a large park, such as found in the National and State parks, an area might develop its own small broadcast studio, and "pipe" programs into the concession lodges and cabin systems during evening hours.

Two-way communication should be used more. A two-way microphone-speaker unit, connected with a monitor at an information desk, would allow visitors to ask questions and receive answers at selected points within a display area. This would be especially effective around historical buildings, archeological ruins, etc. This system can also be combined with a small, fixed T.V. camera mounted to view the area being displayed, the scene being shown on a desk monitor inside the visitor center, museum, etc. This would enable the desk attendant to see the visitor asking the question as well as fix his location.

More attention might well be given to the use of puppets in telling an interpretive story. This is not just a gimmick that children love; adults like it also. A word of caution: not everyone can do this effectively, but when well done, it is a good device.

We might also give more consideration to some of the things we are now doing, hopefully with improvements:

Have more and better demonstrations.

Have devices in our exhibit areas that visitors can activate.

Use better color in displays, and, in most instances, make displays an all-color program. People are used to good color in movies, television, stores, etc.

Plan more interpretive devices for areas away from highways and developed areas.

Make better use of photo points. Usually such points are simply designated as such. These could also contain interpretive messages.

Consider the possibility of using inspirational messages at noteworthy, aesthetic points.

Make better use of museum collections. Too often these turn out to be dead storage. With a little imagination, the collection room can also be used for display purposes.

Devote more attention to youthful visitors. Too many interpretive programs are designed only for adults.

Develop the interpretive possibilities of our streams, lakes, etc.

Develop more underwater facilities for interpretation, such as underwater auditoriums, underwater visitor centers with exhibits, underwater viewing rooms, floating viewing rafts, guided underwater tours, etc.

Obtain a better understanding of the local environment and ecology, and plan ways of presenting this knowledge to the visitor and especially to schools. Environmental awareness is most important today.

Plan ways to make invertebrates better known to the public.

Running a "live" interpretive program is a never ending challenge to the true interpreter. You can be sure of one thing: the more you learn about interpretive methods and techniques, the more you will find that you really don't know nearly enough!